"Amir Tsarfati has crafted a timely and much-needed message to the global Church. His invitation to reconsider Bible prophecy is compelling, biblical and downright fascinating. Tsarfati takes us on a guided tour that ultimately leaves us gazing on the beauty of God's plan. You will not be disappointed!"

Jason Elam, former NFL kicker; special ambassador
for Bible translation, The Seed Company

"Amir Tsarfati is a friend who has given me incredible insight into the fulfillment of biblical prophecy in our day. He loves God's Word, God's Son, God's people—and the land that never ceases to grip the world's attention. This timely book is a well-written, thrilling, thought-provoking, challenging, encouraging must-read for anyone who longs for peace, and hope, in the last hour. The Spirit within me rises up and bears witness that Amir has written truth. Read it."

Anne Graham Lotz, author, *The Daniel Prayer*

"*The Last Hour*, by Amir Tsarfati, is a brilliant, passionate, clarion call for understanding and embracing the accuracy of Scripture. Amir is a gifted scholar who has devoted the majority of his life to a journey through antiquity to current and future times, through the lens of God's inerrant Word."

Kathy Ireland, Bible student; wife; mother;
chair and CEO, Kathy Ireland Worldwide

"I have worked extensively with Amir Tsarfati in my radio and conference ministry. He is a young voice crying in the wilderness, awakening many people—including Millennials—to the importance of the one-third of the Bible excluded from many pulpits and seminaries. I am deeply grateful to Amir for rekindling a passion for understanding the last days not seen since the 1970s. Pay attention to his words in this book. They are outlined in an easy-to-understand writing style, and they

are sure to ignite many more to be looking up and listening for a shout and a trumpet."

Jan Markell, founder/director, Olive Tree Ministries

"Amir Tsarfati is a man I consider to be an insightful teacher and a good friend. He has a deep understanding of the Bible, and his insider view of the Holy Land is unparalleled. I highly recommend the teachings of Amir and his book *The Last Hour* to all who want a greater understanding of what our Lord has planned for the end times."

Senator Emmanuel "Manny" Pacquiao,
world championship boxer; senator of the Philippines

"Here is a biblically solid, passionately written, accurate study in biblical eschatology. The reader can rest assured that what is being presented is sound. What Amir also does in this book is give you glimpses into declassified insights from an Israeli perspective. In addition, you will find his own personal testimony of just how much God's Word means to him and how powerful it has been in his life. I recommend this book with a five-star rating—written by a lifelong friend, a faithful brother and a lover of Yeshua unlike any other I know. You will be edified while reading it."

Jack Hibbs, pastor, Calvary Chapel Chino Hills

THE LAST HOUR

THE LAST HOUR

AN ISRAELI INSIDER LOOKS AT THE END TIMES

AMIR TSARFATI

Chosen

a division of Baker Publishing Group
Minneapolis, Minnesota

© 2018 by Amir Tsarfati

Published by Chosen Books
11400 Hampshire Avenue South
Bloomington, Minnesota 55438
www.chosenbooks.com

Chosen Books is a division of
Baker Publishing Group, Grand Rapids, Michigan

Printed in the United States of America

Library of Congress Cataloging-in-Publication Data
Names: Tsarfati, Amir, author.
Title: The last hour : an Israeli insider looks at the end times / Amir Tsarfati.
Description: Minneapolis, Minnesota : Chosen, a division of Baker Publishing
    Group, [2018] | Includes bibliographical references.
Identifiers: LCCN 2018019488| ISBN 9780800799120 (pbk. : alk. paper) | ISBN
    9781493415243 (e-book)
Subjects: LCSH: End of the world. | Eschatology.
Classification: LCC BT877 .T73 2018 | DDC 236/.9—dc23
LC record available at https://lccn.loc.gov/2018019488

Cover design by Rob Williams, InsideOutCreativeArts

In keeping with biblical principles of creation stewardship, Baker Publishing Group advocates the responsible use of our natural resources. As a member of the Green Press Initiative, our company uses recycled paper when possible. The text paper of this book is composed in part of post-consumer waste.

green press INITIATIVE

20 21 22 23 24 25 26   11 10 9 8 7 6 5

To Miriam, my love

"An excellent wife is the crown of her husband."
Proverbs 12:4 ESV

CONTENTS

FOREWORD

I have known Amir Tsarfati for two decades. I had the privilege of traveling all over Israel with him when I was leading a tour and he was leading the tour guides. Amir has also spoken to the church I pastor in San Diego, California. He is an articulate and passionate supporter of Israel, the land where he was born.

Today, Amir's home overlooks the Valley of Megiddo—Armageddon—which is a constant reminder of the call that God has placed upon his life to teach from the Bible God's plan for the end times. This book is a part of that calling.

I have read hundreds of prophetic books in my ministerial lifetime, but I have never read a book like *The Last Hour*. This is a prophetic book written by a Jewish believer. You can feel the author's passion in his words. What he writes is not literature, it is his life. I am pretty sure that if you strike up a conversation with Amir, you will be talking about the future of Israel within the first thirty minutes.

I read *The Last Hour* in one sitting. I was immediately struck by the author's personal testimony and intrigued by the way the story of God's plan for the Jewish people paralleled the way

God has worked in his own life. Amir's defense of the uniqueness of Israel in God's plan of redemption and his arguments against replacing Israel with the Church leave no room for those who believe that God has forsaken His chosen people.

This book is about prophecy. The history of Israel, both ancient and recent, is at the core of end times truth. Beginning in Genesis chapter twelve with the Abrahamic covenant, we are taken on a journey of both joy and sorrow. Israel's periods of obedience seem to be overwhelmed by her rebellion against God and His prophets. Finally, God sends them their long-awaited Messiah and they nail Him to a cross and go on with their lives.

Pogroms and persecution scattered the Jewish people throughout the whole world. Amir reminds us of their awful suffering and suggests several reasons why, even today, this continues to be their experience. But the author will not let us forget God's promise of restoration, and since you are reading this book, you are alive to witness the fulfillment of that promise. The nation of Israel has returned to her land.

In a powerful speech to the United Nations General Assembly on October 1, 2015, Israeli Prime Minister Benjamin Netanyahu described the miraculous preservation of the Jewish people:

> In every generation, there were those who rose up to destroy our people. In antiquity, we faced destruction from the ancient empires of Babylon and Rome. In the Middle Ages, we faced inquisition and expulsion. And in modern times, we faced pogroms and the Holocaust. Yet the Jewish people persevered.
>
> And now another regime has arisen, swearing to destroy Israel. That regime would be wise to consider this: I stand here today representing Israel, a country 67 years young, but the nation-state of a people nearly 4,000 years old. Yet the empires of Babylon and Rome are not represented in this hall of nations.

Neither is the Thousand Year Reich. Those seemingly invincible empires are long gone. But Israel lives. The people of Israel live.[1]

Israel has been described as "God's time clock," "God's barometer," "God's prophetic clock," "the powder keg fuse for the final world conflict," "the touchstone of world politics," and "the evidence that God is the God of history." In 1948, with the establishment of Israel as a nation, the prophetic clock began ticking.

In the final chapters of *The Last Hour*, the author turns our attention to the 36th through 39th chapters of the prophecy of Ezekiel. Reading these ancient words against the backdrop of what is happening today in Israel gives me the chills. What God has promised to His people, He is fulfilling, and you and I have been privileged to be alive to witness it.

As I finished reading this book, I thought of individuals I want to send it to. Some are believers who are very confused about the future and seem to have lost all interest in reading, talking or knowing about prophecy. This book is thoughtfully written, and it takes what could be confusing and makes it understandable. This is also an evangelistic book, and I believe that God is going to use it to open hearts to the Gospel. Finally, for followers of Christ, *The Last Hour* is a call to action. Time is winding down for the world as we know it today! The prophetic clock is nearing zero.

And do this, knowing the time, that now it is high time to awake out of sleep; for now our salvation is nearer than when we first believed. The night is far spent, the day is at hand. Therefore let us cast off the works of darkness, and let us put on the armor of light. Let us walk properly, as in the day, not in revelry and drunkenness, not in lewdness and lust, not in strife and envy.

1. "Full Transcript of Netanyahu's Address to UN General Assembly," *Haaretz*, October 2, 2015, http://www.haaretz.com/israel-news/1.678524

But put on the Lord Jesus Christ, and make no provision for the flesh, to fulfill its lusts.

Romans 13:11–14

Dr. David Jeremiah, founder and president, Turning Point;
senior pastor, Shadow Mountain Community Church,
El Cajon, California

ACKNOWLEDGMENTS

First and foremost, I want to thank the Lord for how He has carried me along from being a child without family, living apart from Him, to where I am today. He showed me His perfect love when He sent His only begotten Son to die in my place to pay for the things that I have done. This is amazing love!

I want to thank my wife, Miriam, and my four children, who pay the daily price of having me gone so much. They have sacrificed greatly, yet they have never complained and have only shown support and admiration.

I want to thank my team at Behold Israel for their love, support and dedication. H. T. and Tara, Gale and Florene, Donalee and Jeff, Andy and Gail, Trisha and Marc, Wayne and Cyndie, Joanne, Hilary, Nachshon—you and so many others have worked tirelessly behind the scenes and off-camera to allow me to take the Lord's truth out to the four corners of the world.

Thank you to Kim Bangs, Esmé Bieberly and the team at Chosen Books.

Finally, thank you to Steve Yohn for your friendship throughout the writing process.

1

LOOKING BACK
BEFORE LOOKING FORWARD

You may think the story of Israel is in its history; I believe the real story is in its future. Granted, I may be a bit biased. When I stand on the porch of my house, the Valley of Megiddo is spread out below me. The Bible calls it Armageddon—that infamous stretch of land where vast armies will assemble before marching to Jerusalem for the great final battle. It is hard to get the end times out of your mind when that valley is staring you in the face each day with your morning cup of coffee.

I can tell you, though, that as I gaze down into the lush, agricultural beauty of that valley, I have absolutely no fear. Sure, the armies for the culminating battle between good and evil are going to gather in my backyard, but I know that I will not be around to see them. I will be celebrating in the presence of my Lord and Savior, Jesus, enjoying the wonders of His presence and His heavenly surroundings. Because I have studied the

Bible, I have an understanding of what God has planned. That understanding gives me peace.

Ultimately, peace is one of God's goals for us in understanding prophecy, and it is also my goal for this book. It is easy to slip into fear when considering prophecy on a superficial level, but looking more deeply into God's promises gives me peace. When Jesus was about to leave His disciples for the cross, He encouraged them with these words: "Peace I leave with you, My peace I give to you; not as the world gives do I give to you. Let not your heart be troubled, neither let it be afraid" (John 14:27). Was this peace some mystical gift that He bestowed upon them? Did He simply breathe His peace into the room? No, the source of this otherworldly peace is seen in the previous verse: "But the Helper, the Holy Spirit, whom the Father will send in My name, He will teach you all things, and bring to your remembrance all that I said to you" (John 14:26). This perfect peace would come from the truth and wisdom that Jesus had already taught to the disciples and from the great new insights that the Holy Spirit would give to them.

If you are a believer in Christ, there is no reason for you to fear what God has planned for this world. True, some nasty things are coming, but He has not destined His children for wrath. As you read this book, it will become clear that He has a plan for you and the rest of the Church—a plan for celebration and not judgment, a plan for joy and not sorrow, a plan for peace and not fear.

Where I Sit

I once heard a man say that it is important to let people know where you sit before you tell them where you stand. To that end, I believe it is necessary for you to know who I am prior to reading what I believe. God has led me on a unique journey

18

that has made me the man I am and contributed to how I view His Word.

Just as Paul began his letter to the Philippians by giving his credentials—he was "circumcised the eighth day, of the stock of Israel, of the tribe of Benjamin, a Hebrew of the Hebrews" (Philippians 3:5)—I will tell you that I am a Jew, of the tribe of Judah, an Israeli of Israelis. And, also as He did with Paul, God rescued me from depending on the law for my salvation and showed me His marvelous grace.

My father's family originated many generations ago in the Champagne region of France. In fact, our family name, *Tsarfati*, means "French" in the Hebrew language. Eventually, my ancestors moved on to Portugal. Then, in 1492, while King Ferdinand and Queen Isabella of Spain were sending Christopher Columbus off to sail the ocean blue, they also issued the Alhambra Decree, which began the systematic expulsion of Jews from the Iberian Peninsula. Soon after, King Manuel I of Portugal got on the bandwagon, and in 1497, all the Jews in his country were given the boot. That was how my father's family found themselves in Tunisia. After many years in northern Africa, they made their way back home to Israel.

My grandparents on my mother's side were Polish Jews. As we all know, Poland was not a great place for a Jew to live in the 1940s. Rounded up and sent to Auschwitz, they somehow survived the horror of that concentration camp. After the war, as soon as the opportunity arose, they joined thousands of other survivors on a ship bound for Israel. The British government turned them away, however, and the ship was forced to anchor in Cyprus. That was where my mother was born—a refugee baby just a few hundred miles away from the Promised Land.

Due to circumstances that I will discuss later, I ended up in foster care at a fairly young age. I eventually settled into the home of a man who was a high-ranking officer with the Israeli police. His son owned a grocery store, and I immediately began working my first job. I was thankful for the roof over my head and for the food in my stomach, but that was all that they gave to me. There was no love there.

When I reached the age of seventeen, my situation began to feel hopeless. I had no real family, no real future and, to top it off, the girl I was in love with did not even know I existed. Suicide was the best option my teenage brain could come up with, so I planned it out. I had the date; I had the bottle of pills. But when the chosen night came, God stopped me. I just could not do it. It was not out of fear or conscience or some great writing in the sky. He had plans for me, and He was not going to let my teenage depression get in the way.

The day after that close call with death, I was a mess. When I was at my lowest, the Lord chose to show Himself to me, and He did it through my best friend from school. As I was talking with my buddy, I suddenly realized that he was actually a Jewish believer in Christ. (I do not use the phrase "Jewish Christian" because most Jews would consider this to be a contradiction in terms. You are either Jewish or you are a Christian; you certainly cannot be both.) How had I missed his faith before? The idea of a Jewish believer was foreign to me, but also very intriguing. When he invited me to his house for lunch, I readily accepted.

I met his family, and they were all very welcoming and loving. I thought, *So this is what a family is supposed to be.* We all sat around the table for the meal, but before I could start eating, everyone began holding hands. The strangest thing I had ever seen then took place: They all started praying. Right there around the table, they were talking to God like He was their best friend. I was blown away. Where was the prayer book? Where was the ritual? Where was the tradition—the ceremony?

Forgetting the food, I started asking questions. "Why are we holding hands?" "How can you just pray off the top of your head?" "Why do you end all your prayers 'in the name of Jesus'?" A very nice lady pulled me aside and suggested, "Why don't you ask God for the answers to your questions?"

I was floored. *Who am I?* I thought. *Why would God listen to me? Doesn't the Creator God who rules over all things have better things to do than listen to the angry complaints of a suicidal seventeen-year-old?*

That night I could not sleep. So much was churning around in my brain—my past, my future, my family, my faith. Finally, I gave in and decided to follow the woman's suggestion to pray. The problem was I did not know how. *Do I stand? Do I kneel? Should my eyes be open or closed? Do I speak the words out loud or to myself?* Not knowing what else to do, I took a piece of paper and a pencil and wrote this sentence: "God, if You exist, then show me who Jesus is." I taped the paper to the wall, knelt in front of it and did my best to pray. I prayed and I waited. I waited and I prayed. No miracle. No Jesus. No nothing. After a time, exhausted, I went to bed.

The next morning, I woke up to go to work. I had been working since I was twelve—before and after school—doing what I could in my foster family's grocery store. Part of my job early in the mornings was to assemble the various sections of the newspaper to prepare them for selling. As I was putting the parts together, I spotted on one page in big, bold letters the word *Yeshua*, which is the Hebrew name for Jesus. Quickly, I closed the paper back up. I thought I was hallucinating. That woman had said that God would answer my prayers, but . . .

Slowly, I opened the paper, and there again was that wonderful name: *Yeshua*. I was not sure whether to laugh or to cry. As I read the accompanying print, I discovered that for the next two nights a group called Campus Crusade for Christ was going to be showing a film all about Jesus. I thought, *Thank You, Lord. I can't believe You put together a whole film just for me.*

I will never forget that night. *The Jesus Film* had been shot in Israel, so I was seeing all these places I knew, hearing Old Testament references that I recognized, listening to Jesus speak a language that I spoke. This Jesus who had seemed so far from me now felt unbelievably close. I was overwhelmed. At the end of the film, I gave my life to Christ.

Then, with all the boldness of a new believer who wants nothing more than for everyone else to experience the same amazing change, I went back home and declared to everyone, "You are all sinners!" My foster family kicked me out of the house that very night. After ten years of living with them, my newfound faith was more than they could take. There I was, without a home, without a family, without a job but, for the first time in my life, with hope.

Different friends put me up for a short period until the time came for me to fulfill my mandatory military service. Some go into their mandatory service with a knife between their teeth, ready to fight. They cannot wait to get out there and shoot something. As for me, I just wanted to get it over with. Only the thought that I had a new opportunity to share my faith brought any excitement.

I was sent to the armored corps. The idea of riding around in a cramped tank was not appealing, so I asked if there was anything else I could do. They obliged by sending me to a telecommunications course. I soon took charge of the telecommunications for a tank platoon, which consisted of twelve tanks. While there were probably 72 other things I would rather have been doing with my life, this was not the worst way to fulfill my mandatory time.

Just as I was settling into that job, my hand became paralyzed—a strange and frightening thing for an eighteen-year-old. The doctors diagnosed a benign tumor in my hand, and they removed the tumor. While I was recovering in the hospital, I received a note saying that I had been selected to go to officer training. I was shocked. Very few are chosen to go through this training process. Yet here I was, singled out for this prestigious opportunity, when I did not even want to be in the military. There had to be some mistake.

When the military tells you to go, however, you go. Soon I found myself out in a desert training facility, figuring that, at any time, someone would realize I did not belong there and send me back. In the meantime, I determined to enjoy it, keep up my Christian witness and learn all I could. They taught weapons, navigation, combat, command skills and intelligence—all the information needed to be a strong officer.

While I was there, I shared the Gospel every chance I got. I knew it could get me into hot water and possibly cost me the opportunity to complete the training. But the change in me had been so dramatic and had given me so much hope for the future that I could not keep it inside. One day I was called into my commander's office. I knew this had to be it. You were only called in to see the commander if you were in trouble or something really bad was about to happen. I went, nervous but relieved. Finally, I would be sent back to the armored corps to finish out my service; then I could carry on with whatever God had in mind for me next. Instead, the commander said, "Tsarfati, we see great potential in you. We think you could go a long way. Just stop your proselytizing." I was so disappointed. I went in thinking I was about to be kicked out; instead, he complimented me.

I graduated and received my commander pin. In other words, I was trained but did not yet have a rank. That would come after completing professional training in an area that would become my specialty. I learned my specialty when I was summoned to the Ministry of Defense. They told me that I had been chosen to be part of an emerging branch of the military called the

Israeli Military Government in the West Bank. I was sent to the Israeli School for Government, where I was taught Islam, Arabic, the culture of the West Bank, Palestinian history and mentality, and how to govern the population effectively. After I completed this training, I finally became an officer.

Having reported to the headquarters in Ramallah, I was asked where I wanted to serve. Most of the officers coming out of training were very gung ho. They wanted to go where they would see the most action. I went in the opposite direction. I was perfectly happy not to see *any* action. Serving my term in a nice, quiet place where I could study my Bible and share my faith sounded like a fine option to me. I asked, "What is the one place nobody else wants to go—and you don't really do anything?" Immediately, they said, "Jericho." I said, "Sign me up!"

When I left for Jericho, I was actually pretty excited. I love history; I love the Bible; I did not love my military job. Thus, Jericho sounded like the perfect situation. Little did I know what was just around the political corner.

Six months after I took this assignment, a new governor showed up in Jericho. He was a strange bird. He had belonged to a secret military branch of Israeli intelligence called 504. These were the folks who operated agents in Syria, Lebanon, Jordan and anyplace else where we needed a little more information. This man was a spy and an operator of spies, but now he had been promoted out of intelligence and made a governor. There is an old saying, "You can take the man out of the KGB, but you can't take the KGB out of the man." The same holds true with members of the 504.

Once the governor settled in, he set out to find someone among his fifty incompetent officers whom he could trust. He settled on me. After running me through some tests—tests I did not even know I was taking—he summoned me to his office. As I stood there, he put a folder on his desk. "You have two options, Tsarfati," he said. "You can continue to do nothing, and you'll end up being nothing. Or you can decide to do something, and you'll end up being something. If you want to be something, then look in the folder. Just a warning, though—if you read what is inside, you will be the only one in this branch of the military who knows about it. In fact, very few people in the entire country know about it. If you leak the information you read, you'll be spending a long time in jail. So, what's it going to be?"

I asked him if I could pray about it. He knew about my faith and said he would give me a few minutes. I was hoping for a few days, but I took advantage of the brief time and asked the Lord for wisdom. Very quickly, it became crystal clear to me that I had to say yes. God had put me in this unique situation for a reason that He understood, even if I did not. While my life may not have been following the path I had laid out for it, I realized that there are times when you simply have to trust God and step through the doors that He opens.

I opened that top secret folder, and inside I found a draft of the "Jericho and Gaza First" chapter of an agreement that would later be christened "The Oslo Accords." Nobody else had seen this or even knew about it. In fact, it would be months before the Israeli public would find out that, for the first time in history, local Arabs would govern themselves as a "state to be" called Palestine. The full agreement was finally signed at the White House on September 13, 1993, by Israeli Foreign Minister Shimon Peres and Palestine Liberation Organization (PLO) Negotiator Mahmoud Abbas with Israeli Prime Minister Yitzhak Rabin, PLO Leader Yasser Arafat and President Bill Clinton overseeing the event. Israel had agreed to allow the establishment of the Palestinian Authority, gradually turning over to them the governance of the West Bank and the Gaza Strip. This may not seem like much to someone who lives outside of

Israel, but in actuality, it was momentous. Jericho had been chosen to be the first city in the history of planet earth to be ruled by Palestinians.

Now, if you are thinking, "Amir, what are you saying? The Palestinians ruled the land of Palestine for centuries before Israel stole it from them," then just be patient. You will soon come to a chapter where we will discuss the history of the Palestinian people and the naming of the land of "Palestine."

Here I was—a 21-year-old Jewish believer in Christ and a first lieutenant in the Israeli army who wanted nothing more than to do nothing—suddenly being placed in a position to do something of historic proportions with the whole world watching. We have our plans, and God has His plans. Guess whose plans win out?

Soon Palestinian leaders began to visit our military headquarters. The governor gave me the responsibility of showing them around. None of my fellow military personnel could figure out why they were forced to scramble around cleaning everything up just so some Palestinians in civilian dress could take a tour. I was the only one who knew that it was in preparation for giving the whole thing to them.

Eventually, the plan was fully implemented, and Israel pulled out of Jericho. I was put in charge of building a new camp to the south. The transition of authority in Jericho pursuant to the 1994 Cairo Agreement was one of the best examples of how smoothly things could work between Israel and the Palestinians. Unfortunately, it was pretty much the only good example.

During this transition time, my body betrayed me. I worked too much; I did not eat or sleep. Who had time to waste on food and slumber? One day there was a big meeting between the Palestinian Minister of Finance and the Israeli Minister of Finance, along with four generals. I welcomed them, shook their hands, stumbled back to my office and collapsed. Someone heard the noise and found me unconscious. People began working on me, trying to get me to respond. I was evacuated by helicopter and taken to the hospital. Because of the hard work of my fellow officers and the grace of God, I am alive today.

After two weeks recovering in the hospital, I returned to my position. By that time, however, it seemed clearer than ever that the military was not where I belonged. Once the time of my mandatory service was up, I left. When I first entered the service, I was clueless as to what God wanted me to do with my life. By the time my service was over, He had made my path perfectly clear.

All the while I had been in Jericho, I was the official tour guide of the camp. I had the opportunity to lead visiting military and political figures around the base and around the town. Soon I became well-known among both the Israelis and the Palestinians as the guy you wanted to lead your tours. Even today, I have many good relationships with Palestinians that began during my time in Jericho. The history, the people, the Bible—all of these caused me to fall in love with the idea of leading people into the beauty, wonder and truth that are found in my country.

As soon as I left military service, I entered the tour-guide program at Hebrew University. After graduating in 1996, I went to Germany to learn the German language. A few years later, I came to America to study theology. It is impossible to understand Israel without understanding the Bible. The two are inseparable.

Having established my career in guiding tours, I began to make many connections with people from the United States and other nations. This led to opportunities to speak to churches in a number of different countries. In 2001, I was invited to speak in the United States. On September 9, I spoke to a church about the coming threat of Islamic terrorism. Based on the number of tapes sold after the message, it was obvious that nobody really cared.

The next day, September 10, I visited New York City for the first time. As I stood at the top of the World Trade Center, I began thinking about the 1993 bombing in the parking garage that killed six and injured a thousand others. I asked the pastor who was with me, "What's going to happen if something hits these buildings? If these buildings collapse, they will take blocks of other buildings with them." The pastor told me that the buildings had been designed to collapse like a stack of cards, and, as we know, the very next day they did just that.

September 11 was a horrific day for America and for the world. Because of my connection with the Israeli military, I learned a lot more about that day than the average American. I was told about plans that had been thwarted on the West Coast. Planes that were about to take off were grounded by the unprecedented, government-ordered air traffic stoppage. These West Coast terrorists, who had not taken into account the different time zones, found themselves without flights. I heard about cars that were stopped while carrying biological weapons, as well as the plans to take out Air Force One using rented Learjet aircraft. That day was terrible—and it could have been so much worse. Unsurprisingly, when I shared the same message on September 12 that I had given on September 9, the response was very different. People were crowded out into the parking lot.

Where I Stand

All this personal history, all these experiences, all this passion for communicating God's truth coalesced into a desire to wake up the Church, to warn nonbelievers and to speak of the blessed hope that believers have. That is the genesis of my ministry, Behold Israel. That is my heart and my purpose.

In these pages, you will find God's biblical truth. You will not find Amir's truth or some denomination's truth or some culture's truth. While I am Jewish and my ethnicity affects the way I see Scripture, a vast majority of my fellow Jews would disagree one-hundred-percent with what is written in these pages. My Jewish heritage is like seasoning on a steak: It does not change the nature of the meat; it just gives it more flavor.

What is contained in this book comes from years of studying Scripture, living in the land of God's chosen people and teaching about biblical prophecy to tens of thousands of people over nearly two decades. God wants us to know His plans. He has spelled them out very clearly. Dr. Ed Hindson from Liberty University wrote, "Bible prophecy is not written to scare us. It is written to prepare us. God's Word reveals these future events to assure us that He is in control even when the world appears to be out of control."[1] As you ready yourself through studying God's Word in anticipation of Christ's return to take us home with Him, you will soon discover the joy and wonderful peace that come from trusting completely in a God who loves you and who is going to accomplish His perfect will in your life and in this world.

2

God Wants You to Know His Plans

The Bible is so complicated that no one can really understand it." "There are so many different ways to interpret it, how can anyone say that they have the truth?" How many times have you heard either of those criticisms? It is as if the Bible is some deep, dark, nearly impenetrable forest, full of confusing allegories, thorny morality and convoluted history. Few who enter are ever seen again. The only way anyone would dare brave it is with a tour guide who claims to know the way. Typically, each of these self-proclaimed guides seems to be taking different paths through that same forest. They cannot all be right, can they?

If the Bible is truly God's Word to humanity, then many feel that He could have spoken more clearly. Nowhere is this confusion more clearly evidenced than in the realm of prophecy. Spend an afternoon with Daniel's statues and Ezekiel's wheels and John's seals: It is no wonder that some folks just throw up their hands and walk away.

Can the seeming confusion of the Bible in general—and prophecy in particular—be sorted out? Is God really communicating one clear message, and can that one clear message truly be understood by us?

A God Who Wants to Be Known

There are certain things in life that are unknowable: where socks disappear to in the dryer, why women go to the restroom in groups and what in the world the inventor of Vegemite was thinking. Our vast, transcendent God, however, is not on that list.

Our Creator wants to be known by His creatures. He shows Himself to us in creation itself:

> Because what may be known of God is manifest in them, for God has shown it to them. For since the creation of the world His invisible attributes are clearly seen, being understood by the things that are made, even His eternal power and Godhead, so that they are without excuse.
>
> Romans 1:19–20

He has also instilled in us His character:

> For when Gentiles, who do not have the law, by nature do the things in the law, these, although not having the law, are a law to themselves, who show the work of the law written in their hearts, their conscience also bearing witness, and between themselves their thoughts accusing or else excusing them.
>
> Romans 2:14–15

Both nature and conscience can be subjective, though. Otherwise, everyone who saw majestic Mount Hermon, located on the Lebanon-Syria border, would say, "Wow! Isn't God wonderful?" In the same way, there would be little for our lawmakers to argue over because they would all see morality and right and wrong in the same way.

To ensure that we truly get a picture of who God is, He has given us a book—the objective (logical, hard facts) complement to the subjectivity (personal feeling, experience) of nature and conscience. In this book, we find both His biography and His plan for the future. If God were unknowable, then why would He make it so easy to get to know Him?

Of course, we can never know all there is to know about our vast God. If that were possible, He would be a small, finite god—not vast at all. Instead, He has revealed to us just enough to spark our excitement, our intrigue, our imagination, our curiosity. He has also given us just enough to ensure our peace. A wealth of knowledge and wisdom is contained in those "just enoughs," ready to be accessed. In Isaiah, God says, "I am the LORD, and there is no other. I have not spoken in secret, in a dark place of the earth; I did not say to the seed of Jacob, 'Seek Me in vain'; I, the LORD, speak righteousness, I declare things that are right" (Isaiah 45:18–19). God wants to be found. He wants to be known. And the primary way that He has revealed Himself is in the Bible.

Reading an Understandable Bible

One key to understanding the Bible in today's world is to read it in a language one comprehends. Typically, the language people best understand is the one they speak. It would make little sense for an English speaker to try to tackle the Bible in Spanish or Norwegian. Likewise, it makes little sense for people to make sense of a Bible written in antiquated English.

I know I am trampling on some traditions here, but please hear me out. The fact that a Bible translation was written five hundred years ago does not make it inherently better, only older. I once heard the story of a man who told his pastor that he preferred reading the Bible in the King James Version—just the way that Paul wrote it! There is nothing more holy about reading the Bible in words that are hard to understand. God is not offended when His words are translated with a *your* instead of a *thy*. There are many excellent English versions out today (NKJV, ESV, CSB, NASB) that go back to the original Hebrew and Greek for their translations. There is no reason one should have to interpret the Bible's words prior to interpreting its meaning. That being said, if you love the King James Bible, and it is what you are used to, then that is great, too. My encouragement is simply to find a Bible that fits the way you learn and is translated in a way that will keep you engaged and excited about studying it.

Reading the Bible in a language that one can understand, however, does not automatically make it understandable. Even when the words are clear and simple, there are still passages that trigger our "Huh?" reflex. Nowhere is this truer than in the prophetic passages. Some of them are just so bizarre that it causes the reader to wonder if there really can be a right way and a wrong way to decipher them.

The Truth of Absolute Truth

The world today has declared that Truth is dead. Sure, people value truth. They agree that it is better to tell the truth than to lie (unless the lie benefits the hearer or the teller or a third party or the community or the legal defense or the reelection). But big "T" Truth met its death around the same time that people began declaring that God is dead.

Now we live in a world of "what is true for you may not be true for me" and "truth is whatever makes you happy." Like all of Satan's other great untruths, this deception has made its way into the Church. Can you really say that there is just one true way to interpret the Bible? Can you really be that arrogant?

In a word, "Yes."

God made a decision to send His message to the world. This message would be His tangible, objective communication to His creation, filled with everything He wanted them to know about Himself, about creation and salvation, about themselves and their future. Can you imagine God choosing forty different authors from three different continents writing in three different languages over a 1,500-year time span merely to communicate a message of abstractions and generalities that people could read their own truth into? What good would that be? God might as well have sent us a sheet of papyrus with the words "Be good" written on it because that is really the only universally accepted "Truth" contained within the pages of His Word (although, I am sure that even then there would arise a faction of Anti-Goodites that would split the Universal Church of Goodness).

In the high priestly prayer, Jesus asked the Father to "sanctify them by Your truth. Your word is truth" (John 17:17). Earlier, He had said of Himself, "I am the way, the truth, and the life. No one comes to the Father except through Me" (John 14:6). Jesus did not say that He is *a* truth. He is *the* truth. Because of this, His communication to us is Truth. So, if I decipher the message of Scripture one way and you decipher it another way, then either I am wrong and you are right, or you are wrong and I am right—or we are both wrong. We cannot, however, both be right; that is the only impossible option.

Certainly, there are different methodologies of interpretation for different passages—literal, allegorical, poetical, etc. There are also varying applications that can be drawn from those interpretations based on culture, life situation, era and other factors. The writer of Hebrews tells us that "the word of God is living and powerful, and sharper than any two-edged sword, piercing even to the division of soul and spirit, and of joints and marrow, and is a discerner of the thoughts and intents of the heart" (Hebrews 4:12). It speaks directly to the life situation of the reader today, just as it spoke directly to the very different life situation of the reader who read the original manuscript two thousand years ago. The one thing that cannot vary is the underlying, foundational Truth of the message that God sought to communicate to us.

Our God is Truth. Thus, all Truth begins with Him and is based on Him. He gave us the Bible so that we could know the Truth—at least as much as He saw fit to share with us. We can know the Truth about His creation of all things. We can know the Truth about sin and His sacrificial provision for our salvation. We can know the Truth about the meaning of life and our purpose on this planet. And, yes, we can know the prophetic Truth about God's plans for the future of this world.

Prophecy Is Biblical

The Bible, every last page of it, is God's written Word to His creation. All of it is important. Paul writes to his protégé, Timothy, "All Scripture is given by inspiration of God, and is profitable for doctrine, for reproof, for correction, for instruction in righteousness, that the man of God may be complete, thoroughly equipped for every good work" (2 Timothy 3:16–17). That first word *all* is very important. God did not look at His layout for the Bible, think "I've got to boost up My word count a little bit" and then pad it with genealogies, prophecy and the Song of Solomon. All Scripture is purposeful and intentionally included by God.

Nevertheless, the one part of Scripture that Christians tend to avoid is prophecy. There are those who are scared of it;

prophecy seems a little creepy with just the right amount of evil, Satan and Antichrist mixed in to make it a subject that seems better suited to fans of Stephen King than the Word of God. There are others who think it is all a little too weird. Locusts and dragons and angels—oh my! There are still others who think that prophecy is either intentionally or unintentionally too vague to make heads or tails of. How could anyone interpret the more "out-there" portions of biblical prophecy with any sort of certainty? Is it not better to focus on the more "applicable" portions of Scripture?

It is true that speaking on the end times can bring out the nuttier side of Christianity. After one talk that I gave, a very normal-looking gentleman approached and said he would like to talk to me. We sat down and began conversing about God's plan for the future. Our discussion was going quite well until he leaned forward and, in a hushed voice, revealed to me that he was one of the two prophets written about in Revelation 11. I looked at my watch, politely excused myself and made a hasty retreat to my room.

While there may be many reasons to avoid studying prophecy, one overwhelming reason should cause us to give it its due: God wants us to know His plans for the future. Unless we are ready to write off as filler more than a quarter of the Bible, we have the obligation and joy to discover what God has laid out for the end times.

In Isaiah 46:9–10, God says,

> For I am God, and there is no other; I am God, and there is none like Me, declaring the end from the beginning, and from ancient times things that are not yet done, saying, "My counsel shall stand, and I will do all My pleasure."

God has laid out a perfect plan for this world, and rather than keeping this plan to Himself, He has shared it with us.

Only He has the wisdom to create this perfect plan. Only He has the power to accomplish it. And only He has the knowledge needed to spell it out for us in ways that, believe it or not, we can actually understand.

Knowledge Brings Peace

Why would God want us to know the details of His plans for the future? The answer is simple: peace. Some may ask, "Is it not enough just to know that God wins in the end?" Well, yes and no. Yes, the simple knowledge that God is the Last Man Standing in this battle between good and evil gives us a peace that our eternity is safely settled. In this peace, we develop a sense of readiness so that we are spiritually prepared for whatever might happen in the world around us. Yet, this knowledge alone is not enough. If God chose to leave the how-tos of this final victory vague or utterly missing, it would be difficult to feel that perfect peace Jesus has promised us: "Peace I leave with you, My peace I give to you; not as the world gives do I give to you. Let not your heart be troubled, neither let it be afraid" (John 14:27).

Peace comes through faith. I have faith that God loves me and will care for me. I earnestly believe that, as the Creator of all things, He is sovereign over His creation and can do with it as He pleases—even with those forces and people who might be working against Him. I hold passionately to the fact that through faith in Jesus' death and resurrection my eternity is solid with God. These beliefs calm my heart when I am thinking of the future.

But peace also comes through knowledge. Imagine receiving a diagnosis of cancer. I know that, for many of you, no imagination is necessary. Now, imagine the oncologist telling you, "I've got it all taken care of. You don't need to know the details of the process. Just know that you'll be fine." How many of you would respond, "Thanks, Doc," and walk out of the office? Very few. Most would refuse to leave the oncologist's office until the plan of attack was clearly explained and every last question was answered. Only when a clear picture was drawn of the treatment process could we begin to breathe a sigh of relief, knowing that the doctor truly did have the situation under control.

On the night before Jesus was crucified, He explained to the disciples that He was going to die, but He made it clear that His death was not the end of the story. He was going away, but He would come back again. And while He was gone, the disciples would not be alone; they would have the Father watching over them and providing what they needed.

Jesus knew that they needed more than just, "Trust Me, guys, this will all work out." Instead, He said, "These things I have spoken to you, that in Me you may have peace" (John 16:33). God gives us prophecy so that we can have perfect peace.

Confusion Brings Weakness

Paul tells us that "God is not the author of confusion but of peace" (1 Corinthians 14:33). And that is exactly why Satan is so determined to keep us ignorant of the things to come. His desire is for our confusion, our worry and our fear. With knowledge comes peace, and with peace comes the power to serve God and follow Him whatever the cost, knowing that He has us safely in His hands for all eternity.

Confusion, in contrast, is a breeding ground for weakness. This spiritual feebleness is based on a fear of the unknown: What will happen tomorrow, next year or when I die? Hebrews 2:15 compares the "fear of death" to a "lifetime subject to bondage." All you have to do is look at our culture to see how true that is.

We live in a world that is obsessed with never growing old. Skin creams, Botox injections and plastic surgeons all promise that they will take years off our appearance. The medical and para-medical industries will load you up with health regimens and vitamins and supplements all designed to ensure that you fend off death for as long as possible. Of course, there is nothing wrong with doing all we can to care for our health and prolong our lives; our "body is the temple of the Holy Spirit who is in [us]" (1 Corinthians 6:19), and we should treat it with care and respect. If we are motivated to care for our health because of fear, however, then it can quickly turn into a physically and emotionally unhealthy fixation.

When we are afraid, we go into protection mode. Our eyes turn inward. Our inherent "me-nature" goes into hyperdrive. Self-preservation becomes our go-to, a mode diametrically opposed to the way we are called to live. We are so afraid of getting hurt that we become paranoid about offending others, challenging others or taking risks. We are like turtles that have retreated into their shells, making us no better (but a little more fragile) than rocks. When we let self-preservation guide our actions, what good are we to anyone?

God has called us to something more; He has promised us something more.

Jesus tells us that the "thief does not come except to steal, and to kill, and to destroy. I have come that they may have life, and that they may have it more abundantly" (John 10:10). Satan's desire is to throw us into confusion and, thus, steal our peace, hope, joy and usefulness. Jesus' coming provides the antithesis to that litany of loss. The word *abundantly* is a wow word. It means super, mega, gigantic, enormous. An abundant life is a life of passion and purpose, serving and sacrifice, hope and happiness.

This abundant life finds its origin in the work of Jesus Christ on the cross. It is deepened and enriched as we learn more about who God is, what He has done for us and what He has planned for the future.

We Really Want to Know

There is a desire built into each one of us to know what the future holds. Once, as I was walking down Eighth Avenue in Manhattan, I passed fourteen psychics, astrologers, palm readers, tarot readers and a host of other establishments in the span of just a few blocks, all designed to tell people one thing—what the future held for them. They must have been doing good business; that is not cheap real estate!

What is true about this current desire for knowledge was also true in Jesus' day. In the gospel of Matthew, the disciples made known their desire for a peek at what was in store for the world: "Now as He sat on the Mount of Olives, the disciples came to Him privately, saying, 'Tell us, when will these things be? And what will be the sign of Your coming, and of the end of the age?'" (Matthew 24:3).

Jesus had just finished telling them about the coming destruction of the Temple; understandably, the Twelve were concerned. How did He respond to their request? Did He tell them a complicated parable? Did He create a poetic allegory? No, He knew their troubled hearts and their desire to understand, and, since "God is not a God of confusion but of peace," He spelled it out for them:

> Take heed that no one deceives you. For many will come in My name, saying, "I am the Christ," and will deceive many. And you will hear of wars and rumors of wars. See that you are not troubled; for all these things must come to pass, but the end is not yet. For nation will rise against nation, and kingdom against

kingdom. And there will be famines, pestilences, and earth-quakes in various places. All these are the beginning of sorrows.

Matthew 24:4–8

Jesus then went on to tell them about their own impend-ing persecution and martyrdom. He spoke of the rise of false prophets, the abomination of desolation spoken of by Daniel, the Great Tribulation and His own Second Coming. Two thou-sand years later, we may read this passage wishing that Jesus had given us more specifics about the who, what and when. But Christ knew just what the disciples needed, and that is what He gave. He let them know that they would not be left alone. He assured them that the Father was still in control. He promised them a Comforter—the Holy Spirit—who would remind them of all these encouragements when they began to forget.

Two millennia later, when we pick up our Bibles, we hold in our hands exactly what God determined we would need to know about Him, about creation and about our past, present and future. It is all there for us to read, learn and understand. When it comes to prophecy, the waters of learning can get a little choppy, but this does not mean we are destined to sink. It just means that before we begin trying to interpret prophecies, we must lay a solid foundation about the nature of prophecy itself.

3

Understanding
Prophecy: Two-by-Two

The first step to understanding prophecy is to define the term, yet even here there can be confusion. When a prophet prophesies, one of two things may be happening: He or she may either be *forthtelling* a message of God or *foretelling* the plans of God. Both of these definitions are accurate, and both fulfill the calling and role of the prophet. To understand the distinction between these two roles more clearly, let's use the Old Testament prophet Isaiah as an example.

When Isaiah prophesied as a forthteller, he spoke out God's truth in a powerful manner. Often his words were those of condemnation against sinful actions:

For You have forsaken Your people, the house of Jacob, because they are filled with eastern ways; they are soothsayers like the Philistines, and they are pleased with the children of foreigners. Their land is also full of silver and gold, and there is no end to their treasures; their land is also full of horses, and there is no end to their chariots. Their land is also full of idols; they worship the work of their own hands, that which their own fingers have made.

Isaiah 2:6–8

Other times he would, in the name of the Lord, command change among the people: "Wash yourselves, make yourselves clean; put away the evil of your doings from before My eyes. Cease to do evil, learn to do good; seek justice, rebuke the oppressor; defend the fatherless, plead for the widow" (Isaiah 1:16–17). The goal is a return to righteousness and a reconciled relationship with God.

Forthtelling calls people out for their sins—past and present. It warns of potential consequences and often spells out a solution for the predicament. Forthtelling looks like a mom marching her son back up to his room for the third time and telling him that if he leaves again without every piece of clothing picked up and put into the hamper, he will be grounded for a week. Forthtelling looks like a boss calling his perpetually tardy employee into the office and giving him a timely ultimatum. It is a rubber-meets-the-road, come-to-Jesus, straighten-up-and-fly-right warning, typically with the "or else" thrown in.

The other role of the prophet is that of foreteller. Here, the message moves from the past and the present to the future. God grants the foreteller a peek behind the heavy curtain that separates today from tomorrow. Then He expects this prophet to tell his audience just what he has seen, whether he fully understands it or not. Looking forward to the coming Messiah, Isaiah prophesies,

There shall come forth a Rod from the stem of Jesse, and a Branch shall grow out of his roots. The Spirit of the Lord shall rest upon Him, the Spirit of wisdom and understanding, the Spirit of counsel and might, the Spirit of knowledge and of the fear of the LORD. His delight is in the fear of the LORD.

Isaiah 11:1–3

Even today, many of my fellow Jews are waiting for this prophecy's fulfillment, not understanding that it has already been realized with the birth of Jesus.

Through foretelling, God reveals His plans for humanity and for the world. Sometimes these promises can bring fear and anxiety:

> Then I saw a great white throne and Him who sat on it, from whose face the earth and the heaven fled away. And there was found no place for them. And I saw the dead, small and great, standing before God, and books were opened. And another book was opened, which is the Book of Life. And the dead were judged according to their works, by the things which were written in the books. . . . And anyone not found written in the Book of Life was cast into the lake of fire.
>
> Revelation 20:11–12, 15

Other times, the excited anticipation of a prophecy's fulfillment is almost unbearable:

> And I heard a loud voice from heaven saying, "Behold, the tabernacle of God is with men, and He will dwell with them, and they shall be His people. God Himself will be with them and be their God. And God will wipe away every tear from their eyes; there shall be no more death, nor sorrow, nor crying. There shall be no more pain, for the former things have passed away."
>
> Revelation 21:3–4

How incredible that day will be when we will dwell with God, seeing Him face-to-face in all His glory! We know that anything we might imagine about that time pales in comparison to the actuality.

That anticipation is part of God's gift to us. He wants us to know what is in store for the world and what is awaiting us; in this knowledge, we will come to know Him better.

The Near and the Far Fulfillments

Just as there are two types of prophecy, there are two types of prophetic fulfillment—the near and the far. Let's look at Isaiah's prophecy of the virgin birth as an example of this dual nature: "Therefore the Lord Himself will give you a sign: Behold, the virgin shall conceive and bear a Son, and shall call His name Immanuel" (Isaiah 7:14). This is a well-known verse that is often read around Christmas, but if we just focus on the eventual birth of the Savior, we will see only half of the wonderful work God accomplishes through this promise.

For the near fulfillment, look at the immediate context of the verse:

> Now it came to pass in the days of Ahaz the son of Jotham, the son of Uzziah, king of Judah, that Rezin king of Syria and Pekah the son of Remaliah, king of Israel, went up to Jerusalem to make war against it, but could not prevail against it. And it was told to the house of David, saying, "Syria's forces are deployed in Ephraim." So his heart and the heart of his people were moved as the trees of the woods are moved with the wind.
>
> Isaiah 7:1–2

After three generations of kings halfheartedly committing themselves to following God, Judah (the Southern Kingdom) finally crowned a really bad one. In 2 Kings 16, we read of King Ahaz, who set the standard for evil, at least until his grandson

Manasseh came along. As soon as Ahaz took over the kingdom, he turned to idol worship, even sacrificing his own sons in the fire to the false god Molech. As a result, the Lord took His hand of protection off Judah, and they began receiving punch after punch from the surrounding kingdoms—first the Arameans, then the Israelites (the Northern Kingdom), the Edomites and the Philistines. Each took a shot at the king and his diminishing kingdom.

There came a point when the king of Syria and the king of Israel banded together to give the final knockout punch to the southerners. Ahaz knew he had no military might to assemble against this force. He and his people were shaking in their sandals, certain that this was the end. But then God stepped in.

God was not done with Judah quite yet. He sent Isaiah to Ahaz with a message, saying, "Don't worry, Ahaz. The clock has hit zero for Syria and Israel, and it is judgment time. I am bringing the king of Assyria down this direction, and those two kingdoms are about to cease to exist. And, just to ease your mind a bit, I'm willing to give you a sign. Anything you want to see—no matter how big or how small—just ask."

Instead of jumping on this gracious offer, Ahaz demurred: "Far be it from me to put God to the test by asking for a sign" (see Isaiah 7:12). Exasperated with Ahaz's continued disobedience and disrespect, God decided to give him one anyway:

> Therefore the Lord Himself will give you a sign: Behold, the virgin shall conceive and bear a Son, and shall call His name Immanuel. Curds and honey He shall eat, that He may know to refuse the evil and choose the good. For before the Child shall know to refuse the evil and choose the good, the land that you dread will be forsaken by both her kings. The LORD will bring the king of Assyria upon you and your people and your father's house—days that have not come since the day that Ephraim departed from Judah.
>
> Isaiah 7:14–17

Thus, the sign God provided was that a particular young woman, who was at the time still unmarried, would soon marry, become pregnant and have a son. She would give him the name Immanuel, which means "God with us," as a reminder to the people of Judah that, despite their sin and rebellion, God was still watching over them. Little Immanuel would grow, and before he reached the age of accountability, God would use the king of Assyria to bring judgment on Syria and Israel, turning those nations into wastelands.

This prophecy had its near fulfillment just a few years after it was given when the Assyrian king Tiglath-Pileser III, followed by Shalmaneser V, plowed through the doomed kingdoms just as Isaiah had presented. What an amazing account! But that is only half the story.

Fast-forward seven hundred years. A young woman, Mary, unmarried and still a virgin, becomes pregnant. But what seems to be the natural result of sin is, in fact, the supernatural result of God's perfect plan. Mary has been specially chosen by God to bear a child conceived by the Holy Spirit. This baby is to be given a very special name—Yeshua—the Hebrew word for "salvation."

If these circumstances were not bizarre enough, one more tidbit of information is given, a reminder of something written long ago. A virgin giving birth as a sign of God's imminent salvation had been predicted centuries earlier by the prophet Isaiah and then fulfilled soon after when a young woman gave birth to a baby who was a reminder that God was still with Judah. Now, a later and greater fulfillment was coming to fruition: "So all this was done that it might be fulfilled which was spoken by the Lord through the prophet, saying: 'Behold, the virgin shall be with child, and bear a Son, and they shall call His name Immanuel,' which is translated, 'God with us'" (Matthew 1:22–23). One prophecy—two specific and incredible fulfillments.

Not all prophecies have this near and far nature. Daniel's prophetic interpretation of Nebuchadnezzar's "mighty image" dream in Daniel 2 was played out just once in the empires that arose after Babylon's downfall. Most of the apocalyptic visions of John in the book of Revelation will find their realization only once at the end of time. It is important to keep in mind, however, that there may be a greater future realization to each prediction as God continues to roll out history.

The Global and the Regional Tracks

The final prophecy duo relates to the two tracks of prophetic fulfillment: the global and the regional. These tracks refer to the scope of the prophecies and the general direction in which biblical prophecy is moving.

Some prophecies are directed to the whole world. The book of Revelation is filled with descriptions of what will happen on a global scale when God wraps up His timeline as seals are opened, trumpets are sounded and bowls are poured out. This is the global track. In other places, we find prophecies specifically related to individual nations or regions. For example, consider Ezekiel 25–32 with its predictions and laments directed toward Ammon, Moab, Seir, Edom, Philistia, Tyre, Sidon and Egypt. This is the regional track.

As we look at the global track, it becomes evident very quickly that this is not a course directed by countries or world leaders but by spiritual forces. The lead has been taken by "principalities . . . powers . . . rulers of the darkness of this age [and] spiritual hosts of wickedness in the heavenly places" (Ephesians 6:12). This doomsday course was initiated at the very beginning when the serpent tempted Eve with questions not only about God's truth, "Has God indeed said . . . ?" (Genesis 3:1), but also about God's character, "For God knows that in the day you eat of it your eyes will be opened, and you will be like God, knowing good and evil" (Genesis 3:5). Eve gave in, as did Adam, and with that surrender, sin and evil came into the world.

But rebellion against God and a desire to be "like Him" began not with those two human sin pioneers, but with Satan himself, who said, "I will ascend into heaven, I will exalt my throne above the stars of God; I will also sit on the mount of the congregation on the farthest sides of the north; I will ascend above the heights of the clouds, I will be like the Most High" (Isaiah 14:13–14). When the devil, once a beautiful angel, was cast down from heaven, a chain of events began that led to the fall of mankind and to our subsequent redemption provided through Jesus Christ—a plan that God had prepared even before that first act of rebellion. This course now leads to the final judgment of all things.

This global track is evident today in the world as the nations rapidly unite together into one anti-God system. We see this unification in the race for a global economy. The world has become economically linked and dependent on an enormous tangle of treaties, agreements, pledges and aid. Thus, when the economic meltdown comes—and it is coming—it will not just affect certain nations or regions; it will be felt worldwide.

This meltdown is assured first of all because so many governments are printing money like crazy without basing it on anything tangible. Soon, this paper currency will devalue itself to the cost of the paper it is printed on. The current interest rates are also pointing toward a global collapse. They are already as low as they can possibly go; some nations such as Denmark, Japan, Switzerland and Sweden have even adopted the illogical theory of negative interest rates.[1]

A number of countries—Greece, Belarus, Venezuela, Ukraine and Argentina—are already nearing insolvency.[2] While the global economy could sustain the fall of these nations, what happens when the United States, France, Germany or the United Kingdom experience economic collapse? The shock wave will trigger a global economic tsunami.

The global track is also evident in the race for a global government. This desire for a one world government was something that used to be discussed secretly behind closed doors. Now, not only is it accepted as a viable option, but it is praised by many, particularly in the United Nations, as a utopian goal that will result in economic, political and social justice. The European Union, the International Court of Justice (or World Court) and the Kyoto Protocol on climate change are just three examples of how individual nations are gradually giving up aspects of their national sovereignty for the sake of the "greater good."

Finally, the race for one world religion clearly illustrates this global track of prophecy. The worldwide popularity of Pope Francis is truly remarkable. Through his efforts, the Roman Catholic Church's goal of reuniting the global Church, Catholics and Protestants alike, is clearly evident. After all, the word *catholic* means "universal"; thus, we are all by definition part of the "Catholic" Church. Pope Francis's personal appeal and gospel of social justice is causing folks from all corners of Christendom to begin downplaying theological differences and focus instead on working together for the common good. While wonderful things can take place as we serve together more ecumenically on a social level, we must never forget the theological doctrines that make evangelical Christianity unique.

Political correctness and the Church's desire for acceptance have led to a deterioration in the things that make Christianity distinct. The acquiescence to Darwinism and the desire to sync evolution with Genesis 1 are gaining ground within Christian academia and the Church. Scripture is allegorized while unproven scientific theory is lionized. It is better to go with the flow than to be laughed at and mocked as being foolish and old-fashioned.

The deterioration of the Church's distinctiveness is also seen in the watering down of its moral standards. Denomination after denomination has collapsed under the pressure of the LGBT agenda. Heterosexual permissiveness and promiscuity have become the rule rather than the exception.

Many churches are no longer about searchers looking for Jesus; instead, they offer a comfortable, happy place to semi-believers who are looking for good people who like to do good things. Good people doing good things? How could there possibly be anything wrong with that?

Evangelical Christianity's loss of distinctiveness opens the door for a general meld into the squishy theological equivalency of ecumenism. As it is absorbed into culture, the Church will cease to be a light in the darkness. The goal of the global track to create one religion led by one religious leader will be that much closer to fulfillment.

In contrast to the global track, the regional track is more localized and is only led by countries and the leaders of countries. In this track, for instance, we find Russia and its invasion into the Middle East. In the fall of 2015, President Vladimir Putin began testing the waters in Syria to see if there would be any reaction to Russian involvement. Putin first smuggled in four fighter jets, flying tightly under a cargo plane in order to hide from radar (*they learned this little trick from us Israelis when we sneaked into Iraq and bombed their nuclear reactor . . . shhhh!*). When there was no international outrage, Russia forged ahead and within two weeks had another 32 fighter planes as well as 12 assault helicopters inside Syria's borders. As we can see now, this was just the beginning.

Within this regional track, we also discover the absolute irrelevance of America and Europe in the Middle East. In late September 2015, a three-star Russian general went to the American embassy in Baghdad to inform them, in Russian, that they better clear out their troops from certain areas in Syria because the Russians were going to start bombing. He later walked away, having received all his demands. What a humiliation for the once-powerful America! Any influence that the West has had in the Middle East is now gone; the baton has been passed. Unless major changes occur, we must all accept that fact. Even with changes, it may be too late. America is no longer a global power.

In this regional track, we also witness the growing isolation of Israel—a topic that we will treat at greater length later. For now, it is important to understand that the nation of Israel has never been stronger financially or militarily. Yet, we have never been so isolated.

This isolation is why Prime Minister Netanyahu came out so forcefully in his 2015 speech to the United Nations. He made it perfectly clear that no matter what decisions were made in that august body, Israel would do whatever it takes to defend its country and its people. While Israel would much prefer to have international friends, we learned long ago that the only ones we can truly depend on are ourselves.

History is moving forward. God is never surprised, and nothing can go against His will. But what are the plans that God has for Israel and for the world?

4

THE LONG, WINDING ROAD
OF PROPHECY

There are those who have a flawed view of how we got this sinful, fallen world. Rightly, they believe that God created a perfect universe with a perfect earth populated by perfect creatures—and crowned with perfect humanity. But then (unbeknown to God, in their minds), Satan crept into the Garden of Eden and struck. Suddenly, sin came into creation. The devil got one over on God. Perfect creation was no longer perfect. God was left with a mess on His hands that He ultimately had to remedy by sacrificing His own Son, Jesus, on the cross.

While the action in this story is accurate, the depiction of God is not. Satan did not perpetrate the ultimate example of "sticking it to the man." God was fully aware of everything that was going on. While He did not cause Satan's actions or endorse these events, neither was He taken off guard. God created the world and humanity with the full knowledge that we would choose sin over Him.

Before He even said, "Let there be light," He had a plan for our redemption. The apostle Peter tells us that our ransom was purchased "with the precious blood of Christ, as of a lamb without blemish and without spot. He indeed was foreordained before the foundation of the world, but was manifest in these last times for you" (1 Peter 1:19–20). The Lamb of God was identified, and His sacrifice was planned before Adam ever existed, before the Garden of Eden or the earth itself was formed, before Satan himself was created.

As we proceed through this chapter, we need to keep this fact in mind. Nothing that has happened throughout history has caused God to slap His forehead and say, "Oy vey! I didn't see that coming!" God knew that the entrance of sin into the world would demand redemption. He also knew from the beginning that, because of the destructive effects of sin, this perfect creation that He had declared "good" in Genesis 1 was ultimately doomed.

The End from the Beginning

When people want to learn about Bible prophecy, the "end times" is typically what is on their mind. The Church today seems less concerned about the forthtelling aspect of prophecy than the foretelling. This is because we want to know the endgame. We know what the beginning is; now we want to know the end. And we are not alone in this desire for end times answers. This longing to know God's plans goes back to the beginning of the Bible.

In the Torah (the first five books of the Old Testament), the "end times" are talked about four different times. When the patriarch Jacob was about to die, he gathered his sons together to bless them. He began, "Gather together, that I may tell you what shall befall you in the last days" (Genesis 49:1). In Hebrew, those last three words are literally "end of days"—the first time that this phrase is used in the Bible. God also revealed His plan to save the world through these blessings. To his son Judah, Jacob said, "The scepter shall not depart from Judah, nor a lawgiver from between his feet, until Shiloh comes; and to Him shall be the obedience of the people" (Genesis 49:10). In this prophetic dedication, we see God's narrow plan to bless the line of Judah. We also get a glimpse of His much wider, long-range plan to bless the world by bringing forth a Messiah from this son of Jacob.

In the book of Numbers, King Balak of the Moabites hired the prophet Balaam to call down curses upon the Israelites. Three times Balak prepared Balaam for a cursing, and three times Balaam answered with a blessing. Finally, King Balak gave up and prepared to send Balaam home. But God would not let Balaam leave without taking a parting shot at Balak and his people. As he prepared to give some bad news about the future of the Moabites, Balaam said, "Come, I will advise you what this people will do to your people in the latter days" (Numbers 24:14). Again, the Hebrew words here are literally "end of days," and the coming Messiah is subsequently promised: "I see Him, but not now; I behold Him, but not near; a Star shall come out of Jacob; a Scepter shall rise out of Israel" (Numbers 24:17). From the mouth of a non-Jewish, polytheistic prophet, God promised a Savior for all the world.

God fulfills His promises. He promised a Messiah in many places throughout the Old Testament (see Jeremiah 23:5–6, 20; 30:9, 24; Hosea 3:5; Daniel 9:24–27; 10:14). All of these promises were fulfilled in Christ. Even the promises given through Balaam and Jacob were answered specifically. Balaam's promise that "a Star shall come out of Jacob" finds its realization in the gospel of Matthew:

Now after Jesus was born in Bethlehem of Judea in the days of Herod the king, behold, wise men from the East came to Jerusalem, saying, "Where is He who has been born King of the Jews? For we have seen His star in the East and have come to worship Him."

Matthew 2:1–2

Jacob's promise of an eternal king in Genesis 49:10 finds its completion in John's words:

Now I saw heaven opened, and behold, a white horse. And He who sat on him was called Faithful and True, and in righteousness He judges and makes war. His eyes were like a flame of fire, and on His head were many crowns. He had a name written that no one knew except Himself. He was clothed with a robe dipped in blood, and His name is called The Word of God.

Revelation 19:11–13

God is a prophecy fulfiller. When He makes a promise—whether it is for a coming Messiah or regarding the end of time—He will carry it out.

God gives us a heads-up not to frighten us, but to let us know what is coming so that we are ready for it. As I quoted earlier, His goal is not to scare, but to prepare. He wants us to know that His plan is not just for the world, but for each and every one of us. I once watched a television program demonstrating the power of new satellite telescopes. One telescope was able to show astonishing views of the universe—galaxies upon galaxies in all their colorful glory. Then the view turned to the earth, and instead of the vastness of the cosmos, the view was an extremely clear picture of a person lying on a blanket on the ground. The detail from this orbiting satellite was amazing and a little frightening. The picture went out again to the universe, then back to the earth. This time, the view went deeper—down through the eye of the person to the cellular and then the molecular levels.

What a perfect illustration of God's end time plans! His plans will shake the heavens and the earth; all people and all things will be affected. Yet that vast, all-encompassing design takes you into account. You are not just a number. You are not a faceless minion, collateral damage or cannon fodder. God's plan for the world is God's plan for you.

In the Beginning

God's plan has not been without its speed bumps and potholes. In the beginning, God created. Through six days of artistic brilliance, God made the heavens, the earth, light, seas, land, plants, fish, birds and all other kinds of animals. After each new, imaginative release, He declared His creation good.

Then came the crowning glory of His handiwork: humanity. Male and female He created them. Their creation was different from that of any other creature that God had formed. The man and woman received the image of God in them—the ability to think and to reason, to love and to feel emotion. God is an eternal Spirit, and an eternal spirit is what we were given. God looked at us, and, as He did with all other parts of His great creative craft, He declared us good.

Part of the "goodness" of our creation is our ability to be "not good." God gave us something different from what He gave to the rest of His handiwork. He gave us part of Himself— the *imago Dei*, the image of God. To be created in the image of God does not mean that we look like Him. It means that we have been given a spirit; God is Spirit, and He has created us as spiritual beings. Because we are more than just flesh, brain, synapse and instinct, we have the ability to think and reason, to love and hate.

Along with His Spirit, He has given us some of His character. The central essence of God's character is love, for God is love: "He who abides in love abides in God, and God in him" (1 John 4:16). The central essence of love is free will. There can be no love without choice. Forced love is not love. Mindless love is not love. If you program your phone to say "I love you" ten times a day, I can assure you that, despite its words, your phone does not love you. It does not have the capacity to feel love or to choose love.

We are not machines. We have been blessed with the wonderful gift of free will—the ability to make choices. Unfortunately, we have used that gift poorly from the very beginning. Adam and Eve were free to love God or to love themselves, to choose God's way or their own way. They chose their own way.

God created humanity to have a relationship with Him, and humanity rejected that offer. Our disbelief and disobedience created a separation between God and man. The Lord could have saved Himself so much pain and sorrow if He had chosen to remove Adam and Eve from the world, rather than just from the Garden. But God's love is too great for that. Before humanity made the choice to rebel—as He knew we would—the Lord had a plan for our redemption.

Our reconciliation with our Creator would come in the form of a King who would redeem us from our sins and rule righteously one day over all things. God prophesied these things through the patriarch Jacob. When Jacob was an old man in Egypt, he knew his time was close, so he gathered his sons together and blessed each one. When he came to Judah, he promised that the line of Judah would be a royal one. From Judah would come a King whose eternal rule would be over the nations. Jesus Christ, the Lion of Judah, is that King (see Genesis 49:8–12).

This promised King is coming. But what will that coming look like? Once more, we find our answers back at the beginning.

God's Plan Takes a Detour

God created Adam and Eve to have a wonderful freewill love relationship with each other and with Him. What better place to experience this passionate connection than in paradise on earth—the Garden of Eden? Love and location—what wonderful blessings from God!

God's blessing did not stop there. Along with these wonderful gifts, God said to them, "Be fruitful and multiply; fill the earth and subdue it; have dominion over the fish of the sea, over the birds of the air, and over every living thing that moves on the earth" (Genesis 1:28). We find three key elements in this passage. The first is blessing: God gave His special blessing to Adam and Eve. The second is seed: God tells them to be fruitful and multiply. The third is land: They are to fill the earth and subdue it.

These first two humans were set up for perfection, but it was not to be. That pesky little "free will" got in the way. Adam and Eve refused to obey God, and the first two humans became the first two exiles. They were exiled from the Garden and from the presence of God. If that were the extent of the story, it would be a tragedy worthy of Shakespeare. No happy ending—only sorrow and death. Instead, just before the exile was pronounced, God dropped in a glimmer of hope in the form of a powerful promise.

Adam, Eve and the serpent were all in God's "principal's office" listening to the consequences of their sin. While they may have been hoping for simple detention, the verdict was expulsion. Yet, while God was handing down the sentences, He added something unexpected to the serpent's penalty: "And I will put enmity between you and the woman, and between your seed and her Seed; He shall bruise your head, and you shall bruise His heel" (Genesis 3:15). Here we find not only the first biblical prophecy but also the chief reason Satan hates God's prophetic word so much.

God promises enmity between the seed of the serpent and the Seed of the woman. Notice anything unusual when you read this? You should. Last time I studied biology, women did not have the seed; that is the man's provision. Women carry the egg.

While this prophecy is a curse for the serpent, it is a wonderful promise of hope for humankind. But this hope will not come from the seed of man. Something unique must happen to fulfill this promise. When has woman ever been given seed apart from man?

Earlier, we looked at the time when the prophet Isaiah predicted the virgin birth. In that prophecy, he foreshadows the answer to this question: "Therefore the Lord Himself will give you a sign: Behold, the virgin shall conceive and bear a Son, and shall call His name Immanuel" (Isaiah 7:14). A virgin giving birth produces a child born without the seed of man.

As we saw earlier, many years after that prophecy, a young, unmarried woman was found to be pregnant. Her fiancé, Joseph, decided to break his betrothal to her quietly. After all, even two thousand years ago, there was only one way a girl could get pregnant. Before he had a chance,

> Behold, an angel of the Lord appeared to him in a dream, saying, "Joseph, son of David, do not be afraid to take to you Mary your wife, for that which is conceived in her is of the Holy Spirit. And she will bring forth a Son, and you shall call His name Jesus, for He will save His people from their sins." So all this was done that it might be fulfilled which was spoken by the Lord through the prophet, saying: "Behold, the virgin shall be with child, and bear a Son, and they shall call His name Immanuel," which is translated, "God with us."
>
> Matthew 1:20–23

God's plan from the beginning was to send His Son, Jesus, to die for our sins so that the separation caused by humanity's rebellion could be bridged by His work on the cross.

God's Plan: Back on Course

Before we continue, it is important to make clear that this plan is not a new plan. God did not have to scramble to come up with a Plan B when the original plan was thwarted by unforeseen circumstances. God did not watch the events in the Garden, slap His head and say, "Great! What now?" This is a Plan B only in the sense that it is the second plan. God knew that Plan A would go by the wayside with the sin of Adam and Eve. Human will asserted itself in free choice, and free choice chose self over God. So God let the world spin for a bit, washed the earth clean with a one-year bath and then launched phase two of His ultimate plan.

This second phase began with Abram, who lived in Ur, a city located in modern-day southeastern Iraq. Along with his father, Terah, and other members of his family, Abram was living a typical pagan life when God pulled the trigger on His revised plan (see Acts 7:2–3).

> Now the LORD had said to Abram, "Get out of your country, from your family and from your father's house, to a land that I will show you. I will make you a great nation; I will bless you and make your name great; and you shall be a blessing. I will bless those who bless you, and I will curse him who curses you; and in you all the families of the earth shall be blessed."
>
> Genesis 12:1–3

Imagine being in Abram's place. There is no indication that he had ever heard from God before; we do not know if he even knew who the true God was. Then a voice or a vision or a dream came, and this new God told him to uproot himself from all that he held dear. He was not even told where he was going: The exact location was on a need-to-know basis, and Abram did not need to know. Whatever methodology God used for His communication, it was effective. The next thing we read is that the whole family headed off to Haran, the ruins of which you can find in southern Turkey. After a temporary halt, long enough for Terah, the family patriarch, to die, Abram packed up his wife, Sarai, and his nephew Lot and hit the road again.

At first blush, this new plan with Abram may seem very different from God's original plan with Adam. It is not. While the recipients are different, the key elements remain the same.

The first element is blessing. God promised that He would take this wandering nobody and make his name great. How many billions of anonymous people have lived and died? Lives were lived, good things were done, fortunes were earned and nations were led by people whose existence has slipped into the void of historical irrelevance. Yet, God promised Abram that people would still be talking about him for millennia to come.

Not only would Abram be blessed, but others would be blessed through him—another hint of the coming Messiah. And if that was not enough blessing to go around, God promised Abram that he would be a catalyst for blessing. If people blessed Abram, God would bless them back. If people cursed Abram, then they'd better watch their backs.

The second similarity between the plans for Adam and Abram was the seed promise. Adam was told to be fruitful and multiply. Abram was promised that he, too, would father a people—a statement that likely caught this aging, childless man a little off guard. Notice the decrease in the size of the blessing, but the increase in the impact. Adam was the father of all people. Abram was the father of a great nation. Yet, it was through Adam that the world was cursed, and it was through Abram that all peoples would be blessed.

To emphasize the magnitude of this great promise to Abram, God gave him a rechristening. No longer would he be called Abram—"father is exalted"; instead, he would be known as Abraham—"father of a multitude." A childless old man, well past fatherhood years, with a wife well past motherhood years, is given a name that, outside of God's miraculous hand, would be absolutely ludicrous. What seems impossible to us is possible with God.

The third element of the blessing, land, also brings a comparison between the first man and the first patriarch. To Adam the whole earth was given, and he was told to fill it and subdue it. Abraham was only given a small portion of land on the east bank of the Mediterranean. But, while Adam's lot was bigger, Abraham's lot was the land of promise—the home of the city where God Himself dwells, the place where Immanuel walked the earth, the scene of the Savior's death, resurrection and ascension, the location where the Great Judge will return to His creation and the site of the eternal reign of the King of kings and Lord of lords.

God's Plan for the Priesthood

Just as God's original plan for a relationship with humankind began with Adam but was fulfilled through Abraham, God's plan for the priesthood began with Adam but was fulfilled by other means. While the prophet is the communicator of God to the people, the priest is the communicator of the people to God. Because of his close relationship with his Creator, Adam can be seen as the first high priest.

In fact, there are numerous parallels that can be seen between the Garden, the home of Adam, and the Tabernacle, the home of the priesthood. In the Garden, we see "the LORD God walking in the garden in the cool of the day" (Genesis 3:8). In the time of the Tabernacle, the Lord promised, "I will walk among you and be your God, and you shall be My people" (Leviticus 26:12). In Genesis, cherubim guarded the entrance to the Garden. When the Tabernacle was built, cherubim were embroidered on the great veil between the holy place and the holy of holies, guarding the entrance to the place where the Spirit of God dwelled.

Speaking of entrances, both the Garden and the Tabernacle were entered into from the east. As for the roles given to them by the Lord, God took Adam "and put him in the garden of Eden to tend and keep it" (Genesis 2:15). The Lord later used those same Hebrew words when He commanded the Levites:

> And they shall attend to his needs and the needs of the whole congregation before the tabernacle of meeting, to do the work of the tabernacle. Also they shall attend to all the furnishings of the tabernacle of meeting, and to the needs of the children of Israel, to do the work of the tabernacle.
>
> Numbers 3:7–8

When it came to clothing Adam and Eve after they sinned, "the LORD God made tunics of skin, and clothed them" (Genesis 3:21). In Hebrew, the word for *garment* (often translated "tunic") is the same one that God used when He told Moses, "Then you shall take the garments, put the tunic on Aaron, and the robe of the ephod, the ephod, and the breastplate, and gird him with the intricately woven band of the ephod" (Exodus 29:5). God designated the apparel for both the first man and the first priest.

In Adam, God began the first priesthood. But Adam failed, and the priesthood was passed on. The second recipient of this priesthood was the nation of Israel. We usually think of the tribe of Levi as the nation's priests, but that was not God's original intent. The Lord says, "Now therefore, if you will indeed obey My voice and keep My covenant, then you shall be a special treasure to Me above all people; for all the earth is Mine. And you shall be to Me a kingdom of priests and a holy nation" (Exodus 19:5–6). It did not take long for the nation of Israel to prove themselves unworthy of this priesthood. All it took was some gold, a little fire and, in the words of Aaron, "This calf came out" (Exodus 32:24). Consequently, God took the priesthood from the people of Israel and gave it to the one tribe that did not take part in the rebellion against the Lord—the tribe of Levi.

God's plan for the priesthood was always much bigger than one tribe of one nation. The Aaronic priesthood was both necessary and beneficial for its time, but it was most definitely just for its time. When Jesus came, He brought a new priesthood that would extend to all of God's people. Being of the tribe of Judah, Jesus could not serve in the traditional Levitical priesthood of the Jews, so He instituted a new priesthood: "For He testifies, 'You are a priest forever according to the order of Melchizedek'" (Hebrews 7:17).

This Melchizedekian priesthood finds its genesis in Genesis. When Abram returned from a successful battle, he was met by an unusual figure, Melchizedek, the king of Salem. This powerful man, to whom Abram offered a tithe of the booty he gained in battle, also bore the designation of "priest of God Most High" (Genesis 14:18). It is this priesthood—the one to whom the father of the Jews offers homage—that Jesus Christ instituted at His incarnation. As the High Priest of this new priesthood, He offers to all believers the right to be priests under Him.

The apostle Peter reveals to us this wonderful new role we have in God's kingdom:

But you are a chosen generation, a royal priesthood, a holy nation, His own special people, that you may proclaim the praises of Him who called you out of darkness into His marvelous light; who once were not a people but are now the people of God, who had not obtained mercy but now have obtained mercy.

1 Peter 2:9–10

God formed the Church into a new people—a new nation—and He has given us the blessing of being able to communicate directly with Him. We do not need a middleman, nor do we need a priesthood. We *are* the priesthood.

Far too often I hear people saying, "Oh, how I wish I were a Jew." Really? Look at the history of the Jews; it is not one that will cause many to feel envy. Yet there are those who attend Messianic congregations, follow the feasts and keep the dietary laws. In fact, many are so committed to their non-Jewish Jewishness that they begin to frown upon those who do not adopt their way of thinking. They are a new breed of Judaizers. Paul made it clear in Galatians 5:12 how he felt about anyone who adds a single rule to the purity and simplicity of the Gospel: "I could wish that those who trouble you would even cut themselves off!"

For members of the Church to seek to become more Jewish is to abdicate their calling. Because of the fall of the Jews, salvation came to the Gentiles. Now it is the role of the Gentiles to deliver the true Gospel back to the Jews. Paul wrote, "I say then, have [the Jews] stumbled that they should fall? Certainly not! But through their fall, to provoke them to jealousy, salvation has come to the Gentiles" (Romans 11:11). The Church is called to provoke the Jews to jealousy, not to be provoked by the Jews to jealousy.

People will sometimes say to me, "Amir, you are not Jewish enough." Is it because I do not follow the Old Testament law? Is it because, before I eat bacon, I sprinkle water on it and say, "You're a chicken! You're a chicken! You're a chicken!"? If following the Old Covenant is what makes you a Jew, then there will be no Jews in heaven, because there is no one, Jew or Gentile, who can fully keep the law. Jesus came to institute the New Covenant, fulfilling the ways of the Old. There should be no identity crisis within the Church over not being Jewish. The Jews have only a thin layer of priests while, in the Church, all are priests. Why would you want to go back to a lesser degree?

God's Plan for the Savior

When Adam and Eve rebelled against God, punishment quickly followed. But when God was meting out just sentences for each member of the spiritual mutiny, He did not start with the two humans. He began with the instigator, the serpent:

> So the LORD God said to the serpent: "Because you have done this, you are cursed more than all cattle, and more than every beast of the field; on your belly you shall go, and you shall eat dust all the days of your life. And I will put enmity between you and the woman, and between your seed and her Seed; He shall bruise your head, and you shall bruise His heel."
>
> Genesis 3:14–15

As soon as this prophecy was pronounced, Satan was put on the defensive. The devil is anything but stupid. He understood that this promise of the woman's Seed meant doom for him. As a result, the enemy has tried for millennia to accomplish an impossible task: cut off the Seed of the woman.

If there is anything we can compliment Satan on, it is his persistence. He tried to stop the Messiah from coming, and he failed. He tried to stop the Church through persecution, and he failed. Now, he is trying to infiltrate the Church with a twisted sort of "If you can't beat 'em, join 'em" plan, and, sadly, he is starting to find some traction.

Infiltration would not have been necessary if the enemy had been able to succeed at any other point along the way. He began his attack on the Seed of the woman by attacking the literal seed of Adam. There was Cain, and there was Abel—a bad guy and a good guy. Satan simply incited the bad guy to kill the good guy. Mission accomplished! But then came Seth.

When the Hebrews were in bondage in Egypt, it was a perfect opportunity to cut off the Seed. Satan prompted Pharaoh to kill all the Hebrew males. Great plan, except one child slipped through the reeds into the protection of the house of Pharaoh. This child, Moses, would eventually lead the Hebrews to freedom.

Many years later, the Jews were captive under the rule of Xerxes, the king of Persia. Satan got hold of a prideful, weak-willed man named Haman. Through the intrigues of this human pawn, the enemy caused a decree to spread throughout the empire that on a particular day all the Jews were to be slaughtered. It was a great plan, until a brave young woman stepped into the picture. Esther, the new queen and a Jew herself, laid a trap for Haman. He promptly stepped into it. The Jews were saved, Haman was not and Satan was thwarted again.

Five hundred years passed, and now it was too late. The Seed had been born. All Satan's plans were unable to stop that from happening. But did he give up? Again, the enemy was persistent. He lost the battle to stop the birth of the Seed, but, if he could keep the Seed from growing, then he still had a chance to win the war. King Herod, a petty, jealous tyrant, was just the man he needed. Because of Herod's insecurity over his throne, Satan was able to cause the monarch to issue an order, based on the words of the Magi, to kill all the male children of Bethlehem aged two years and under. Never mind the collateral damage,

Herod and Satan would have their baby. Just before the order was issued, an angel appeared to Joseph and said,

> "Arise, take the young Child and His mother, flee to Egypt, and stay there until I bring you word; for Herod will seek the young Child to destroy Him." When he arose, he took the young Child and His mother by night and departed for Egypt, and was there until the death of Herod.
>
> Matthew 2:13–15

Another near miss, another failure for the enemy.

Now the Seed—the Savior—was grown, and the devil was forced to change tactics. Up until this point, his goal had been to destroy everyone and anything in order to prevent this very situation. It was too late to stop the Seed from coming, so he had to make sure that the Savior was not allowed to fulfill His saving role. The destroyer was forced into the role of preserving the one life that must be sacrificed so that all lives might be saved.

When Jesus and His disciples were in the district of Caesarea Philippi, He asked them who they thought He was. Peter, speaking through the power of God, replied, "You are the Christ, the Son of the living God" (Matthew 16:16). When Jesus affirmed him for his answer, Peter's head began to swell a bit. Later, when the Lord began explaining to His disciples that He would go to Jerusalem to be abused, killed and on the third day resurrected, Peter rebuked Him: "Far be it from You, Lord; this shall not happen to You!" (Matthew 16:22). Jesus' response was swift and harsh: "Get behind Me, Satan! You are an offense to Me, for you are not mindful of the things of God, but the things of men" (Matthew 16:23). To whom was this rebuke leveled? Not to Peter, but to Satan. Jesus knew who was really speaking. The enemy did not want Jesus to die because he understood that his ultimate defeat would come when Jesus defeated death through His resurrection. Another demonic plan utterly failed.

The devil was in panic mode. God's perfect plan of reconciliation had been bought and paid for; His free gift of salvation had been put in place. All that was left for the devil was to create as much havoc as he could before his ultimate doom came. We will see later how much destruction his deceptions are causing to the nations of the earth. But his final day is drawing closer. With that expiration date looming, the only hope Satan has is to put it off for as long as possible.

How is it possible for Satan to delay his final judgment? He has got to find a way to beat the system, so he has determined to use God's Word against Him. Satan knows the Scriptures, and he understands the prophecies that must be fulfilled. Just prior to the Second Coming of Christ (the catalyst that will usher in the final period of the devil's freedom), Romans 11 promises us that all Israel will be saved. But what if there is no Israel to be saved? If the nation is eradicated, the prophecy cannot be fulfilled, and Christ cannot return to take His rightful throne on the earth. This is another reason why the enemy has been so determined to destroy God's chosen people.

Through the horrors of World War II, one out of every three Jews was killed. The enemy used every tool at his disposal, including a long-standing, deep-seated anti-Semitism that tainted much of Central and Eastern Europe. Yet God did not allow His people to perish from the earth.

Satan, however, has not given up. Another Holocaust, even more lethal than the first, is coming.

> "Awake, O sword, against My Shepherd, against the Man who is My Companion," says the LORD of hosts. "Strike the Shepherd, and the sheep will be scattered; then I will turn My hand against the little ones. And it shall come to pass in all the land," says the LORD, "that two-thirds in it shall be cut off and die, but

one-third shall be left in it: I will bring the one-third through the fire, will refine them as silver is refined, and test them as gold is tested. They will call on My name, and I will answer them. I will say, 'This is My people'; and each one will say, 'The LORD is my God.'"

Zechariah 13:7–9

Two-thirds of the Jewish people will be wiped out. It is hard to imagine that kind of devastation. But even with two out of every three Jews being slaughtered, Satan still does not have a victory. God will preserve one-third. They will be the ones suffering through the Tribulation, and they will be the ones who will recognize Jesus as their true Messiah at the end. Once again, the Lord manages to show His grace and mercy in the midst of tragedy.

God's plan will prevail; His Word will be fulfilled. While prophecy is not always pretty and may even cause us to wince at times, there is such peace in knowing that God is in control, no matter how things around us may look.

5

Israel: Still God's Chosen People

Rejection is an ugly experience—especially if you are a kid, especially if it comes from your parents. My parents always had a rocky marriage. My dad came from an Orthodox Jewish environment. The rules and structure turned him off to religion, and that struggle expanded to many other areas of his life.

My mom had two issues that plagued her. The first was the Holocaust trauma of her parents. Horror like that does not end with those who experienced it. The trauma is passed down through generations in attitudes, fears and emotional scarring. A second issue stemmed from the death of her brother. During the War of Attrition with Egypt, he was stationed on the warship *Eilat* in the area of Port Said. The Egyptians fired a torpedo that hit the *Eilat*, sinking her and killing many who were aboard, including my uncle. This tragedy affected her greatly. With two dysfunctional parents who were still struggling with the long-term emotional fallout of the Holocaust, my mother felt that her brother was the only one to whom she was truly close.

When I was two years old, my parents' marriage fell apart. Not surprisingly, this had a huge impact on my sister, my brother and me. My mother was not stable enough to care for all three of us on her own, so my father gained custody of me and my brother. After a while, we moved in with an aunt, but that only lasted for a time. At the age of eight, I was placed in foster care along with my brother. There were long-lasting ramifications of this separation from my parents. While I do have a relationship with both of them today, it is distant.

The first foster family I was with was a catastrophe. Terrible abuse occurred in that home, and I was finally removed. I was taken in by another foster family and lived with them for the next ten years. This is the family that I mentioned in the first chapter. It was a blessing to have a place to live, but that was not the same as having a home and a family. I experienced another kind of rejection when this family threw me out of the house after I dared to share my newfound faith in Christ.

I do know what it feels like to be rejected—to have people turn their backs on you and walk away. As I look at my own children, I cannot imagine doing that. Even the imperfect love that I feel for them and for my family would ensure that I could never cut them off or abandon them.

This parental abandonment, some say, is exactly what God has done to the nation of Israel. At times, He speaks of the Jews as a husband speaks of his wife. At other times, He speaks of the Jews as a father speaks of his children. How could God, whose love is perfect and so much greater than mine, forever turn His back on those who are His own?

Why Did God Choose Israel?

Why, out of all the nations of the earth, did God choose Israel? Why not a larger nation—or a more obedient one? Why not a nation that knows how to play a little better with others?

Why Israel?

People have tried to answer this question for centuries. They have postulated theories, devised scenarios and constructed great towers of reason and logic. The problem with all of this "brilliant" thinking is that the wrong question is being asked.

Why Israel? There is no great answer for that. The question we should be asking is "Why did God *choose* at all?"

The reason for the choosing lies not in the one chosen, but in the Chooser. Besides, when you start asking God "Why?" questions, you may suddenly find yourself in deep water. The next thing you know, God is asking "Where were *you*?" questions, and you are repenting in dust and ashes—just ask Job.

God's act of choosing, also called His "election," is purely an outflowing of His sovereignty. He saw, He determined, He chose. This means that election is in no way performance-based. There is nothing that Israel did that caused them to be the chosen nation. They were not holier, wiser, wealthier, more powerful or more fun to be around. In fact, when God chose Israel, "they" were just "he"—one man, Abraham—an exile without a nation or any land. He had not accomplished any great feats; he had not conquered any despots or slain any dragons or done anything else worthy of note. Abraham's election was all about God and His divine plan.

Because there was nothing that Israel did to become "the elect," there was also nothing they could do that would cause them to become the "unelect." Election, otherwise, becomes a matter of performance. If you are good, you stay elected. If you are bad, you become unelected. This human-centric election is not what we find in Scripture. Election is a matter of God's will—from beginning to end.

So, why Israel, rather than any other people or nation? In Romans 9, Paul takes us back to the birth of Abraham's grandsons. Rebekah, Abraham's daughter-in-law, was pregnant with twins. It was a rough pregnancy, and the babies inside her seemed to be constantly battling. She was so troubled by this that she asked God for an explanation. His response is fascinating: "And the LORD said to her: 'Two nations are in your womb, two peoples shall be separated from your body; one people shall be stronger than the other, and the older shall serve the younger'" (Genesis 25:23).

Before these children were even born, God announced that He had determined to break customary conventions and elevate the younger son over the older. Why? Because He chose to. Paul used even stronger language when speaking of these two brothers: "As it is written, 'Jacob I have loved, but Esau I have hated'" (Romans 9:13).

The apostle then goes on to address the accusation that it is unjust or unfair for God to choose one over the other:

> What shall we say then? Is there unrighteousness with God? Certainly not! For He says to Moses, "I will have mercy on whomever I will have mercy, and I will have compassion on whomever I will have compassion." So then it is not of him who wills, nor of him who runs, but of God who shows mercy.
>
> Romans 9:14–16

God elected Israel to be His chosen people because He is God. In His wisdom, compassion, mercy and deep, unending love, He determined that this man, Abraham, would be the father of the nation that He would one day call His bride (see Jeremiah 31:31–32; Hosea 2:16, 19–20).

Why Did God Choose Anyone?

God is the Creator of all things, and He has a passionate love for His creation. In one of the most famous verses of the Bible, we are told, "For God so loved the world that He gave His only begotten Son, that whoever believes in Him should not perish but have everlasting life" (John 3:16). If God loves the whole world, then why did He feel it necessary to designate one nation as special or unique?

To answer this question, we need to go back to the reason God created humanity in the first place. Anyone who has studied the seventeenth-century "Westminster Shorter Catechism" will be quick with this response: "Man's chief end is to glorify God, and to enjoy him forever."[1] God created us so that we would, in turn, glorify Him.

To glorify someone does not just mean to praise them or speak well of them. We glorify God through how we live and how we praise Him; these two elements together make up what is true worship. Because both of these aspects need to be present, Scripture never speaks of non-Christians glorifying God. Certainly, there is a future time when God promises, "As I live, says the LORD, every knee shall bow to Me, and every tongue shall confess to God" (Romans 14:11, quoting Isaiah 45:23). But the knee-bowing and tongue-confessing refer to a time when all will be judged. Many will realize too late how wrong their rejection of God was during their lifetime.

For God to be glorified, true believers in Him must do the glorifying. For there to be believers in Christ, there must also be those who direct people to Him. This was the mission of the Jewish people—and God's reason for making a choice in the first place.

Paul, taking words from Isaiah 52, wrote,

> How then shall they call on Him in whom they have not believed? And how shall they believe in Him of whom they have

not heard? And how shall they hear without a preacher? And how shall they preach unless they are sent? As it is written: "How beautiful are the feet of those who preach the gospel of peace, who bring glad tidings of good things!"

Romans 10:14–15

Israel was to be the shining light, the beacon on a hill. This is so important for us to understand. Israel was not chosen for its own sake, but for the sake of the rest of the world. Isaiah wrote, "I, the LORD, have called You in righteousness, and will hold Your hand; I will keep You and give You as a covenant to the people, as a light to the Gentiles" (Isaiah 42:6). Later, the prophet again recorded, "It is too small a thing that You should be My Servant to raise up the tribes of Jacob, and to restore the preserved ones of Israel; I will also give You as a light to the Gentiles, that You should be My salvation to the ends of the earth" (Isaiah 49:6).

God had a purpose for Israel to fulfill in His overall strategy to create glorifiers. Once that purpose is ultimately fulfilled, there will no longer be a need for a distinct Israel. The nation will have completed its calling. That has not yet happened. As Paul writes, "For I do not desire, brethren, that you should be ignorant of this mystery, lest you should be wise in your own opinion, that blindness in part has happened to Israel until the fullness of the Gentiles has come in" (Romans 11:25). Even today, the impact of the historical people of Israel is being used by God to bring Gentiles (the rest of the world) to Christ.

Tools in the Hands of the Builder

When I lead tours in Israel, we are always sure to make a stop at one of the many olive wood stores. There, visitors can find beautifully carved figurines depicting anything from Moses and the Ten Commandments to the Israelite spies carrying a giant cluster of grapes on a pole to a detailed replica of the Last Supper. Few leave the stores without purchasing at least one of the hundreds of lovely Nativity scenes that are offered in all sizes and prices. The beauty of these souvenirs is particularly remarkable when you consider the raw product from which they are carved.

The olive tree is a gnarled and tangled sight. When measured against the symmetry of the oak, the character of the willow or the majesty of the redwood, the pitiful olive tree pales in comparison. But that is just to the untrained eye.

Let the artisan examine an olive tree, and he will see not what is, but what can be. He knows that hidden under the thick, craggy bark is a beautifully marbled wood. The skilled craftsman will take what looks like nothing to the layperson, set to work on it with his tools and create a marvelous work of beauty.

Before you get too far ahead of me, I need to let you know that Israel is not the "marvelous work of art" in this illustration. While it is true that the analogy of making something wonderful from materials that others would cast away may also fit the Jewish people, in this context, God is the Craftsman, Israel is the assortment of tools and the Church is the beautiful work of art. Without God masterfully using Israel on the world of the Gentiles, the Church would not be what it is today.

What were the tools that God used?

First of all, the law was given through the Jews. While many see the law and grace as antithetical to each other, the two actually go hand in hand. Paul tells us that it was necessary for the law to come so that we could see that we are sinners: "I would not have known sin except through the law. For I would not have known covetousness unless the law had said, 'You shall not covet'" (Romans 7:7). The law was given to direct people to Christ.

It took the law for the world to know that God does expect a standard of behavior from His people. When we deviate from that standard, there are consequences—primarily in our relationship with God: "For the wages of sin is death, but the gift of God is eternal life in Christ Jesus our Lord" (Romans 6:23). The law shows us that we have a sin problem that needs a solution. The solution is Christ Jesus our Lord.

No Israel, no law. No law, no awareness of the sin problem. No awareness of the sin problem, no apparent need for Christ. While it is true that we are no longer under the law today, it took the law—and Christ's fulfillment of it—to bring us to this point of freedom:

> For when we were in the flesh, the sinful passions which were aroused by the law were at work in our members to bear fruit to death. But now we have been delivered from the law, having died to what we were held by, so that we should serve in the newness of the Spirit and not in the oldness of the letter.
>
> Romans 7:5–6; cf. Matthew 5:17

A second Jewish tool that the Master Craftsman used to create the Church was their belief in one God. Monotheism (mono = one; theos = god) was the original spiritual worldview. In Eden, Adam and Eve were not with the Lord God "walking in the garden in the cool of the day" (Genesis 3:8), while spending the rest of their time with various other gods who happened to be passing through. From the beginning, there was a belief in just one God.

The population grew and spread, however, and Satan started doing his thing. Soon the idea of multiple gods took hold, and, apart from a little window of time following the Flood, polytheism has never let go. Abraham himself was living a polytheistic life until the one true God called him to follow.

Moses emphasized the singularity of the Deity when he wrote the *Shema*, the beginning of the most beautiful and powerful prayer in all of Scripture: "Hear, O Israel: The Lord our God, the Lord is one!" (Deuteronomy 6:4). This bold conviction, declared to a polytheistic world, set Israel apart from all other nations. This monotheistic faith laid the foundation for Christianity and the incredible concept of a single God being manifest in three persons—the Father, the Son and the Holy Spirit.

In one final way God used Israel to shape the Church, for through this frustratingly rebellious nation, we are able to see the depth of His love and grace. Throughout the history of Israel, a continual cycle of sin/punishment/repentance/forgiveness/restoration occurs. This nation, who had seen the one true God work powerfully so many times and in so many ways, always seemed to be wanting to find a reason to follow other gods. The prophets often used the illustration of an unfaithful wife straying from her husband to underscore the severity of this rebellion. Ezekiel 16 takes it even further, showing Israel not just as a wife who has abandoned her husband for another, but as one who has taken up prostitution. When that lifestyle did not satisfy her, she began paying others to sleep with her. The story is harsh, ugly and definitely R-rated. But in the end, we see God taking her back—forgiving her, renewing His covenant with her, loving her.

This story of God's powerful grace is repeated throughout the Old Testament from Hosea to Jonah to Isaiah. In fact, it is very rare to find a prophetic passage where God promises punishment without also extending the hope of restoration.

One of the most beautiful pictures of God's amazing grace occurs in the five chapters of the book of Lamentations. The prophet Jeremiah was distraught as he witnessed the destruction of Jerusalem by the Babylonian armies of King Nebuchadnezzar. His horror and despair were channeled to his pen, and he wrote a tragically beautiful series of poems. He managed to hold himself together through the first two songs of sorrow, but he became overwhelmed during the third. It was too oppressive, too heartbreaking. So, he threw out a lifeline, and God caught hold of the other end.

> This I recall to my mind,
> Therefore I have hope.
> Through the LORD's mercies we are not consumed,
> Because His compassions fail not.
> They are new every morning;
> Great is Your faithfulness.
> "The LORD is my portion," says my soul,
> "Therefore I hope in Him!" . . .
> For the Lord will not cast off forever.
> Though He causes grief,
> Yet He will show compassion
> According to the multitude of His mercies.
> For He does not afflict willingly,
> Nor grieve the children of men.
>
> Lamentations 3:21–24, 31–33

After this reminder of the never-ending love of God, Jeremiah was able to return again to face the destruction of the Holy City, secure in the knowledge that God does not abandon that which is His own. The history of Israel teaches us this wonderful truth.

Can you imagine parents "unadopting" a child? That is precisely what some people believe God did to Israel. Surely they were so wicked and rebellious that God finally had enough; they had surpassed the limits of His grace and forgiveness. Scripture tells us otherwise. Both in the Old and New Testaments, we see a God who never lets go.

I know what it is to feel abandoned by one's parents. I know the pain and fear of feeling like you are on your own. With my God, I will never be on my own. He has adopted me as His child, and He will never kick me or anyone else out of His family.

The spiritual history of Israel should be an incredible encouragement to Christians. When we sin and rebel, He will bring discipline—and that may make life unpleasant for a while. But when we finally come to our senses and turn back to God, He will be there with open arms, like the father of the Prodigal Son, waiting for His child to come home to Him (see Luke 15:20).

Is Israel Still Chosen by God?

Israel was chosen by God for a special relationship. Out of that relationship came a special purpose: to direct people to Jesus Christ. We have just reviewed how God used them effectively to carry out that goal. So what about Israel now?

One popularly held belief, particularly within the Reformed tradition of the Church, is that God is done with Israel. There are two schools of thought here. There are those who believe that Israel's constant rebellion took God to His limits, and that their ultimate rejection of the Messiah was the last straw. Supersessionism, more commonly known as Replacement Theology, typically inserts the term *Church* whenever Israel is mentioned in the New Testament after Pentecost and gives to the Church the covenants of the Old Testament.

A second, somewhat milder view arises out of Covenant Theology. This view states that God never intended for Israel to be a permanently distinct entity. From the time of Abraham, God viewed the nation as the Church. When the Old Covenant was supplanted by the New Covenant through Jesus' work on the cross, the Church finally was able to break from her national identity and become the one people of God, made up of Jew and Gentile, that she was always intended to be.

Whether Replacement or Covenant, the resulting view of modern Israel is the same: It is a nation like every other nation. While it may be beneficial from a geopolitical point of view to support Israel, from a spiritual perspective, the Church should feel no connection or loyalty. Adherents quickly point out that these are ancient traditions going back to the early Church. This is quite true. The movement to remove Israel from the plans of God was born in the first century. The apostle Paul saw it and rebuked those who believed it.

Paul understood quite clearly the rebelliousness of Israel. They had the law; they had seen the works of God firsthand. Israel only existed as a nation because of His countless interventions, yet they still turned their backs on Him. After using the words of Isaiah to commend the Gentiles for accepting the truth of the Savior, Paul wrote, "But to Israel he says: 'All day long I have stretched out My hands to a disobedient and contrary people'" (Romans 10:21).

Those words sound pretty bleak for this upstart nation. But Paul knew from the beginning that his words might be completely misunderstood and misinterpreted, especially by those who already had anti-Jewish presuppositions. That is why, if you read on, Paul makes it clear that people should not be too quick to write off Israel:

> I say then, has God cast away His people? Certainly not! For I also am an Israelite, of the seed of Abraham, of the tribe of Benjamin. God has not cast away His people whom He foreknew.
>
> Romans 11:1–2

God has not rejected His people. Paul could not have made this clearer. Israel exists as a unique people group with a special relationship with God and a distinct part in His plan.

Some have argued that there cannot be a distinct plan for Israel because salvation is not through the law but through Jesus Christ. To this I say, "Exactly!" The Jews have a special relationship with the Lord and a distinct plan, but not a separate path to salvation. Everyone is saved through an individual acceptance of what Jesus did on the cross. Jews are not saved by following the law. Jews are not saved because they are Jews. They are, however, the only people who will experience a national salvation. This salvation will only come when revival spreads among the Jews who survive the Tribulation and individually commit themselves to the Lord. For those who doubt this eventuality, Paul wrote,

> For I do not desire, brethren, that you should be ignorant of this mystery, lest you should be wise in your own opinion, that blindness in part has happened to Israel until the fullness of the Gentiles has come in. And so all Israel will be saved.
>
> Romans 11:25–26

There could not be a clearer answer to those who think that God has forsaken His people.

How did this misunderstanding of God's relationship with Israel begin? We can only speculate. Perhaps it was a backlash to the Judaizers of the first-century Church. That particular group of Jews held to the belief that for Gentile believers the cross was not enough; they also needed to follow the Mosaic Law, particularly in the areas of circumcision and food laws. This works-based heresy spread rapidly through the Church, creating the need for a special council to be held in Jerusalem to discuss it. At this meeting of many of the apostles and leaders of the fledgling Church, Peter stood up and confronted those who were trying to saddle the Gentiles with the Mosaic Law:

> Now therefore, why do you test God by putting a yoke on the neck of the disciples which neither our fathers nor we were able to bear? But we believe that through the grace of the Lord Jesus Christ we shall be saved in the same manner as they.
>
> Acts 15:10–11

In other words, if the Jews themselves could not keep the law, why would they expect the Gentiles to be able to? Salvation comes through God's grace alone.

The way the Jews treated the Gentiles in the early days of the Church may have caused some resentment. Perhaps plain old anti-Semitism was also behind the desire to remove the Jews from the plans of God. In any case, from the time of Abraham, there has never been a period when Israel was not hated and reviled. The first century was simply the first time that people were able to give this hatred a biblical guise. Add to that historical disdain the Jews' sense of national superiority, and a pogrom was waiting to happen.

Consider this. Why is the United States of America loved by some and hated by many around the world? Because God has given it a unique and wonderful place in history. He has blessed it with enough wealth and power to exert its influence throughout the globe. That alone causes jealousy among other nations. Combine this with the attitude of exceptionalism held by the average U.S. citizen, and the resentment grows.

The first-century Jews had forgotten that they were exceptional only because of who God had made them to be. Simply put, they began believing their own press. John the Baptist confronted this arrogance when, seeing the Pharisees and Sadducees, he said, "And do not think to say to yourselves, 'We have Abraham as our father.' For I say to you that God is able to raise up children to Abraham from these stones" (Matthew 3:9). Gentiles looked at this self-declared exceptionalism and truly resented it.

Unfortunately, the reputation the Jewish people have as being arrogant and aloof is not without its foundations. God formulated their national exceptionalism, and they became conceited in it. When Jesus came along and called them out, telling them that they were missing the point of their calling and challenging them to do better, they got rid of Him.

Their resistance to changing their attitude and embracing the true nature of their calling can be seen in an event that took place just prior to Jesus' crucifixion. According to tradition, the Roman governor would release a prisoner at Passover. Pilate offered the Jews a choice. One choice was Jesus, whose name means "God saves." He was the only Son of the Father, come to lead the world to truth. The second man was also named Jesus—"God saves"—with the last name of Barabbas—"son of the father."

Two men—both reminding us that God saves, both sons of the father. And of these two men, the Jews chose to release the one who would not ask them to change, the one who would not challenge their presuppositions and would let them remain arrogant and aloof.

Israel is definitely responsible, in part, for their reputation. This is not to say that the Jews have deserved the mistreatment that they have received over the millennia. Only the persecutor is responsible for acts of persecution. Just as the Jews neglected to recognize that God, not their inherent uniqueness, was the reason they were chosen, so too did the Gentiles of the Church. An arrogance and superiority resulting from being of the New Covenant fueled Gentile resentment toward those of the Old Covenant.

Paul saw this danger growing in the Church. He addressed it using the illustration of an olive tree. Many of the Jews—the original branches on the tree—were removed through unbelief, while the Gentiles were grafted in. Out with the old, and in with the new. In the event that these new branches began thinking they were special, supplanting the old guard, Paul admonished,

> And if some of the branches were broken off, and you, being a wild olive tree, were grafted in among them, and with them became a partaker of the root and fatness of the olive tree, do not boast against the branches. But if you do boast, remember that you do not support the root, but the root supports you.
>
> Romans 11:17–18

Rather than being resentful or disdainful of its Jewish roots, the Church should celebrate its origins.

The Dangers of Misunderstanding Israel

Despite the clarity that Paul brings to the question of Israel's continued election, many still reject this truth. It is difficult not to see the hand of the enemy in this blinding of certain segments of the Church. From the beginning, Satan has sought to destroy the Jewish people. When he found that was impossible, he tried a different route: to make Israel irrelevant. This marginalization took strong root through the allegorical hermeneutic of Origen (third century), was cemented into the Church through Augustine (fourth century) and was nailed into the Reformation through Martin Luther (sixteenth century).

Throughout history, God has said to His people, Jew and Gentile alike, "Give Me a reason to bless you, and I will!" He said this to the Jews during the time of the judges; He said this when "He came to His own, and His own did not receive Him" (John 1:11); and He said this every time you find a "but" or a "yet" among the Old Testament prophets.

To understand God truly, we must have an accurate understanding of the people of Israel. An accurate understanding means we do not think either too little or too much of them. It is as theologically unsound and doctrinally dangerous to think that Israel is nothing as it is to think that Israel is everything.

I once spoke to a pastor who was very Israel-centric. His whole ministry was wrapped up in keeping the feasts and studying the law. As we talked, he told me that he believes there is a dual covenant for salvation. While Gentiles are saved through the work of Jesus on the cross, Israel does not need Jesus because of its special status before God. What a dangerous heresy!

This pastor is not alone in his thinking. In December 2015, the Vatican's Commission for Religious Relations with the Jews released a paper entitled "The Gifts and the Calling of God Are Irrevocable." In this paper, the Roman Catholic Church makes clear their belief that Jews can be saved without believing in Jesus Christ:

> That the Jews are participants in God's salvation is theologically unquestionable, but how that can be possible without confessing Christ explicitly, is and remains an unfathomable divine mystery.[2]

Once the necessity of Jesus can be removed from one people, it can be removed from others. One of the Vatican's key strategies is to make everyone part of the Catholic Church; as mentioned earlier, the word *Catholic* means "universal." This effort, cast in the politically correct guise of ecumenism, particularly by the current head of Catholicism, Pope Francis, puts the focus on the gospel of the Beatitudes, rather than on the true Gospel. It is a social gospel—a works system that feels good and costs little. And it is the foundation of the one world religion that will be ushered in during the end of time.

It is truly a great danger to think too highly of Israel, but it is equally dangerous to think too lowly. If the Church disregards the Jewish nation, it will miss its responsibility to God's chosen people. Just as Israel had a duty toward the Church, as we have seen above, so does the Church have a duty toward Israel.

This duty is manifest in two ways. First, the Church must provoke Israel toward jealousy. While not a custom in Israel, dating is a very important part of courtship in many other cultures. Imagine a girl and a boy are dating; let us call them Sue and Benny. The problem is that Sue does not treat Benny very well. She is always flirting with other guys, ignoring Benny and talking badly about him. Sue figures that she can get away with it because she is Benny's girl, and Benny is so loyal that even a golden retriever could learn a thing or two from him. Then, one day, a new girl catches Benny's eye. New Girl respects him and treats him well. Abruptly, life changes for Sue. Benny and New Girl start spending time together, and Sue is on the outside looking in. She realizes how good she had it with Benny. She sees that somehow his life has managed to move on without her, and she wants nothing more than to win him back.

This is Romans 11. Israel's treatment of God has been abysmal. As the Lord turns His attention to the Church, Paul's hope and prayer is that the Jews, seeing that they are no longer the apple of His eye, will realize their error and long to win back their place of favor.

> I say then, have they stumbled that they should fall? Certainly not! But through their fall, to provoke them to jealousy, salvation has come to the Gentiles. Now if their fall is riches for the world, and their failure riches for the Gentiles, how much more their fullness! For I speak to you Gentiles; inasmuch as I am an apostle to the Gentiles, I magnify my ministry, if by any means I may provoke to jealousy those who are my flesh and save some of them.
>
> Romans 11:11–14

Rather than turn her back on the people of God's chosen nation, the Church must pray that Israel will see what it is missing by not relying on the simple Gospel of grace through faith. The Church's desire should be to stoke the passion Israel once had for God so that they will return to their first love. Once shaped by Israel, the Church has become the tool that the Master Craftsman uses to craft something new out of His original elect people.

The Church's second duty is found later in Romans. As Paul closes his letter, he speaks of his future plans. Although he would have loved to visit the Roman church, he has other obligations:

> But now I am going to Jerusalem to minister to the saints. For
> it pleased those from Macedonia and Achaia to make a certain
> contribution for the poor among the saints who are in Jeru-
> salem. It pleased them indeed, and they are their debtors. For if
> the Gentiles have been partakers of their spiritual things, their
> duty is also to minister to them in material things.
>
> Romans 15:25–27

Life was very difficult for the Jewish believers in Christ living in Jerusalem. The persecution was great, which made food
scarce. The Gentile churches heard of the need and jumped in
to help. The reasons for coming to the Jews' aid are interesting.
First, they were pleased to do it. They saw brothers and sisters
in Christ in need, and they were happy to sacrifice for them.
Second, they owed it to the Jerusalem believers. Because the
spiritual blessings of the Gentiles came from the Jews, they realized that the Jews should receive material blessings from them.

This debt still stands today. Israel unlocked God's spiritual
blessings. Through the Jews, He gave His truth to the world.
This is a timeless doctrine. Neither have these spiritual blessings ended; in fact, they are renewed with each new believer
who responds to the truth that God revealed through the Jewish nation. As a result, the Church has a duty to support Israel
financially.

I am not saying that the Church is obligated to send checks
every month to the Israeli government. But if there is no Jewish
ministry included in a church's mission budget, they are not fulfilling their spiritual obligations. This is true of the individual
Christian as well. All Gentile Christians should be financially
supporting either a ministry to Jews or a ministry run by Jews.
There are many excellent ministries that are truly doing God's
work. Through prayer and some online research, Christians can
easily separate the wheat from the chaff. This is obedience, and
it is true worship through giving.

Israel, the Church's Spiritual Litmus Test

The nation of Israel was chosen by God to lead people to Christ. As time progressed, the Lord moved the Jews from being primarily a chosen people to being a choosing people. The emphasis is no longer on their uniqueness but on their need to choose God for their salvation. Their election does not save them; their decision to commit to Christ does. The New Testament makes this clear.

The Church has taken an opposite path. Individual believers move from being a choosing people to being a chosen people. As individuals choose to give their lives to Jesus, they become part of a new nation:

> But you are a chosen generation, a royal priesthood, a holy nation, His own special people, that you may proclaim the praises of Him who called you out of darkness into His marvelous light; who once were not a people but are now the people of God, who had not obtained mercy but now have obtained mercy.
>
> 1 Peter 2:9–10

The mission of Israel to lead people to Christ has now been given to the Church.

Has Israel fallen out of favor with God? Yes. Has God rejected His elect nation? Absolutely not. Has God stopped loving His chosen people? Never. The Church must never stop loving the Jewish people either.

How the Church treats Israel is a litmus test of its temperature, readiness and doctrine. A rejected Israel reveals a sick Church. You cannot love God and hate that which God loves. If you hate that which God loves, you will end up loving that which God hates. Lord, protect Your Church from that fate.

6

THE DECEPTION
OF THE NATIONS

Nobody likes to be deceived. That moment when you discover that someone has been pulling the wool over your eyes is both embarrassing and angering. *I should have seen it,* you chide yourself. *How did I miss it?* No matter how hard we try to evaluate truth and discern people's motives, sometimes we simply get taken in.

Sadly, no one is surprised anymore when the media is discovered acting with intentional deception. That dishonesty is rarely seen more clearly than in the media's handling of Christianity and Israel. They truly are the "Medianites"—always fighting against God and His people. These Medianites are not acting of their own accord, however. They are being used.

As we saw before, Satan is a deceiver, and his goal is to deceive the nations. Jesus said of him, "He was a murderer from the beginning, and does not stand in the truth, because there is no truth in him. When he speaks a lie, he speaks from his own resources, for he is a liar and the father of it" (John 8:44). Today, one of the greatest tools he has to carry out his plans is global media. Whether it is print, the internet, or the airwaves (after all, Satan is called the "prince of the power of the air" [Ephesians 2:2]), the enemy is a master at getting his lies into the eyes and ears of the world's population.

In March 2015, Israelis went to the polls and reelected Benjamin Netanyahu as prime minister. People around the world were shocked. Why could Israel not get rid of this hard-liner? Did they not want to be accepted by the world? Did they not want peace and security? Hope and prosperity? The reelection of Netanyahu could only mean continued alienation from the West and danger from all around.

At least, that was what the media was saying. And the more the media said it, the more people believed it. A lie, repeated often enough, eventually gains traction. Satan is not concerned with the truth; he desires victory. And he has like-minded accomplices in today's media to help him accomplish that goal.

The truth is that Israel has never been healthier. It has never been in a better position financially or security-wise. Manufacturing and agriculture continue to grow, and the fairly recent discovery of vast amounts of natural gas has made the nation a world player in the energy field.[1]

The media sold the lie that despair and fear are all you find in Israel, and the nations bought into it.

The Master Deceiver

To deceive is to know the truth but to choose to tell people otherwise. If you do not know the truth and say something that is untrue, then you are simply wrong. Speaking an intentional untruth, however, makes you a deceiver.

Satan knows the truth. He knows who God is. He has seen His infinite power at work; he knows the Bible and understands his ultimate end. There are no glimmers of hope for him. There are no "what ifs" or strategic plays that can bring him to ultimate victory. Any hope, purpose, peace or meaning that he offers to the world apart from God is intentional deception. Any distractions he uses to draw people away from God or promises he makes of a fulfilling, self-satisfied life are evil, pure and simple. Satan knows his final destination, and he is determined to take as many with him as possible.

Satan deceives individuals in order to draw them away from God. He also has larger deceptions that operate on a global scale—a duplicitous metanarrative that he is foisting on the world. These global deceptions fall into two categories: the deception of the world and the deception of the nations. The deception of the world has to do with the rise of a global economy, a global religion and a final world leader all will follow. We will deal with these matters in the chapters to come.

For the moment, let us focus on the deception of the nations. While differentiating between *world* and *nations* may seem like splitting hairs, in Scripture, there is a major difference. When the Bible speaks of the *world*, it refers to all nations, including Israel. *Nations*, however, signifies only those countries that are not Israel—the Gentiles, the *goyim*.

Isaiah wrote of the time when Satan's arrogance got the best of him. Frustrated that someone of his power and beauty should be relegated to number two, Satan made a power play, but he completely underestimated God. The Lord thwarted his plans and, as punishment, banished this chosen cherub from heaven. Lamenting this tragedy, Isaiah wrote, "How you are fallen from heaven, O Lucifer, son of the morning! How you are cut down to the ground, you who weakened the nations!" (Isaiah 14:12).

The enemy has debilitated the Gentile nations by selling the lie that God is done with Israel. As we will see later, there is a price to pay when countries turn their backs on the chosen ones of God. More than ever, the rest of the world is choosing to abandon Israel. When decisions are based upon a lie, a person or a nation will become weak.

The deception wrought by the devil has permeated the world for generations past, and it will continue until almost the end of time. Following the Second Coming of Christ, there will be a brief respite from Satan's lies:

> Then I saw an angel coming down from heaven, having the key to the bottomless pit and a great chain in his hand. He laid hold of the dragon, that serpent of old, who is the Devil and Satan, and bound him for a thousand years; and he cast him into the bottomless pit, and shut him up, and set a seal on him, so that he should deceive the nations no more till the thousand years were finished. But after these things he must be released for a little while.
>
> Revelation 20:1–3

Satan will be bound and thrown into the bottomless pit for a thousand years. Why does God do this? So that the enemy might not deceive the nations any longer. This millennium of truth and peace is described in glowing terms throughout the Bible, but it all comes to an end the moment the deceiver is released. Unsurprisingly, his first act is to deceive the nations once again.

Deception #1: Israel Is Not God's People Anymore

Satan is the master deceiver, and he is the deceiver of the nations. This deception extends to all nations, except Israel. How do we know? Because Israel is the primary subject of the deception. In fact, only Christians and Jews can see the falsehoods that the deceiver is foisting for what they are: Christians because their truth comes from the Word of God and the wisdom of the Holy Spirit—Jews because their blindness is of a different type and from a different Source. The apostle John, using the words of Isaiah, lays the responsibility for the Jews' confusion squarely at the feet of God's sovereignty: "He has blinded their eyes and hardened their hearts, lest they should see with their eyes, lest they should understand with their hearts and turn, so that I should heal them" (John 12:40).

The deception of the nations regarding Israel takes five different forms. The first is the claim that Israel is not God's people anymore. We will only take a short time with this because it has already been explained at length in the preceding chapter.

God told Israel, "For you are a holy people to the LORD your God, and the LORD has chosen you to be a people for Himself, a special treasure above all the peoples who are on the face of the earth" (Deuteronomy 14:2). They are a specially chosen people, intimately and protectively loved by Him: "For thus says the LORD of hosts: 'He sent Me after glory, to the nations which plunder you; for he who touches you touches the apple of His eye'" (Zechariah 2:8). The apple of one's eye refers to the pupil—completely surrounded by the iris and protected by the lashes—indicating something or someone essential and of great value. Just as Israel has been cherished by God.

But Satan has convinced the nations that God has forsaken His people. Even many Jews have bought into this lie. My own grandparents, having survived the horrors of Auschwitz, could not believe that there was still a God who loved the Jewish people. As a result, Israel has looked elsewhere for protection. If God is not on our side, they reason, then we need to look to America or somewhere else for our safety.

Historically, this is what the Jews have tended to do. When Israel was facing the Assyrian Empire in the eighth century BC, they turned to Egypt for aid rather than seeking God's help against this seemingly insurmountable foe: "Woe to those who go down to Egypt for help, and rely on horses, who trust in chariots because they are many, and in horsemen because they are very strong, but who do not look to the Holy One of Israel, nor seek the LORD!" (Isaiah 31:1). God wants to help; if only His people would turn to Him rather than to the world. As Isaiah wrote, God's love is a deep, eternal love—a passionate and protective love:

> But Zion said, "The LORD has forsaken me, and my Lord has forgotten me." Can a woman forget her nursing child, and not have compassion on the son of her womb? Surely they may forget, yet I will not forget you. See, I have inscribed you on the palms of My hands; your walls are continually before Me.
>
> Isaiah 49:14–16

Now, you may say, "But that is the Old Testament. We need the New Testament. We are Christians. We believe in Jesus. After all, Jesus was not Jewish; He was a Christian." Well, I have bad news for you. Jesus was as Jewish as they come, and He never preached from the New Testament once! Be that as it may, God is the same yesterday, today and forever. The God who made those loving professions in Isaiah is the same God who led Paul to write, "I say then, has God cast away His people? Certainly not!" (Romans 11:1). He has neither forsaken nor forgotten His people.

This should give us great comfort. If God were able to forget His people, then He would be able to forget you and me. But our God is an eternal God who makes eternal promises and establishes eternal relationships. When we give our lives to Him, we are safe and secure in His arms throughout eternity.

Deception #2: The Land's Real Name Is Palestine

It is time for some lab work. Go to your bookshelf or bed stand or wherever you keep your Bible. Turn to the back where the publisher has put the maps. Thumb past the patriarchs, the twelve tribes, the kingdom under Saul and David and the divided kingdom until you come to the New Testament period. What is the title of the map that shows first-century Israel? Chances are that it reads, "Palestine in the Time of Jesus." The problem is that there was no such thing as "Palestine" during the time of Jesus.

Christ was born in the land of Israel. When His family returned from Egypt after fleeing Herod, they returned to the land of Israel as we see in the book of Matthew:

> Now when Herod was dead, behold, an angel of the Lord appeared in a dream to Joseph in Egypt, saying, "Arise, take the young Child and His mother, and go to the land of Israel, for those who sought the young Child's life are dead." Then he arose, took the young Child and His mother, and came into the land of Israel.
>
> Matthew 2:19–21

Even when the Old Testament prophet Ezekiel looked to our modern times, predicting the return of Israel to the land, he wrote,

> Then He said to me, "Son of man, these bones are the whole house of Israel. They indeed say, 'Our bones are dry, our hope is lost, and we ourselves are cut off!' Therefore prophesy and say to them, 'Thus says the Lord God: "Behold, O My people, I will open your graves and cause you to come up from your graves, and bring you into the land of Israel."'"
>
> Ezekiel 37:11–12

Never in Scripture do we see the name Palestine being used.

Where, then, did the name come from? In AD 132, a Jewish man named Simon bar Kokhba led a revolt against the Roman Empire. Starting in the central town of Modi'in, the revolt quickly spread. Hadrian, like most Roman emperors, did not take too kindly to uprisings, so he dropped the hammer on Judea. Nearly one-third of the Roman army, under the leadership of General Julius Severus, descended mercilessly upon the nation. The country was devastated, and over a half million Jews lost their lives. Because this was not the first revolt of this rebellious people, Severus decided to ensure they would not rise again—so he stripped the country of its identity. No longer would the country of Judea exist; it would be called Syria-Palestina instead, which was eventually shortened to Palestine.[2]

The name *Palestine* is derived from the Philistines. "Aha!" some may say. "There is our Arab connection." Not so fast. The Philistines were not Arabs, but sea people. In fact, the root of their name comes from the Hebrew word for "invade." So, if anyone has invaded the land, it would be "the Invaders," not those to whom God originally gave the land.

Palestine immediately became the accepted name for the region, and the name Israel was soon forgotten—precisely what the enemy wanted. In a call for the Lord to rise to action, the psalmist Asaph wrote,

> For behold, Your enemies make a tumult; and those who hate You have lifted up their head. They have taken crafty counsel against Your people, and consulted together against Your sheltered ones. They have said, "Come, and let us cut them off from being a nation, that the name of Israel may be remembered no more."
>
> Psalm 83:2–4

Outside of the Church, this very thing has happened among the nations.

Even the late nineteenth- and early twentieth-century Jews who first returned to the land seemed to forget the land's true identity, calling themselves Palestinians. Prior to the 1948 independence, *The Jerusalem Post*, a Jewish newspaper, was *The Palestine Post*. The Israeli Philharmonic, a Jewish orchestra, was called the Palestine Orchestra. When there was a call to arms among the repatriated Jews to fight in World War II, they organized as the Palestinian brigade. If anyone has a right to the Palestinian name, it is the Jews—not the Arabs.

This confusion has led to a delegitimizing of the nation of Israel throughout the Arab world and beyond. There is no international organization that has been more of an enemy to Israel than the United Nations, a body that claims to represent the world's opinion. Instead, they are quick to tout the cause of a nation, Palestine, that never really existed, and of a people who have no true national identity.

Deception #3: The Arabs Were There First

The land on which the state of Israel currently exists is not, nor ever has been, Arab. Many say that the Jews are invaders, driving the Arabs off their ancient lands. The Palestinians' whole identity is centered on being the victims of a great cultural crime perpetrated by the illegitimate nation of Israel. The question really comes down to who has the right to call that land their own.

To answer this question properly, we must go back to the identity of the original owner. David tells us, "The earth is the LORD's, and all its fullness, the world and those who dwell therein. For He has founded it upon the seas, and established it upon the waters" (Psalm 24:1–2). God is the Creator of all things, and the Creator has full rights over His creation; this includes the right to give portions of His creation to whomever He chooses:

And the LORD said to Abram, after Lot had separated from him: "Lift your eyes now and look from the place where you are—northward, southward, eastward, and westward; for all the land which you see I give to you and your descendants forever. And I will make your descendants as the dust of the earth; so that if a man could number the dust of the earth, then your descendants also could be numbered. Arise, walk in the land through its length and its width, for I give it to you."

Genesis 13:14–17

There is one thing we can be sure of in Scripture: God means what He says. When He says forever, He means *forever*.

When the Hebrews were in slavery in Egypt, the Promised Land belonged to them; they just needed to take possession of it. When they eradicated the Canaanites, Hittites, Amorites, Perizzites, Hivites and Jebusites from the land, they were within their rights to do so because it was their land given originally to Abraham by God. When the Northern Kingdom of Israel was absorbed into the Assyrian Empire and the Southern Kingdom of Judah was exiled to Babylon, the land still rightfully belonged to the Jews. When Zerubbabel, Ezra, Nehemiah and all the other exiles returned to the land, they were returning to their homeland. Land, once given by God, cannot be taken away by man.

Thus, in the late nineteenth century and throughout the twentieth century, when members of the Jewish Diaspora began returning from all over Europe to the ancient land of their people, they were not invading another people's country. They were coming home to the land that God had promised would be theirs forever.

Another aspect of this deception is the idea that the Jews drove out the Palestinians from a thriving country. Nothing could be further from the truth. In 1867, not long before Jews began resettling in the land, Mark Twain visited the region with a group of fellow travelers. He published a diary of sorts from his adventure in a book called *The Innocents Abroad*. He described the land as a "desolate country whose soil is rich enough, but is given wholly over to weeds—a silent, mournful expanse."[3]

Twain is not a man you would want to hire to promote tourism, but his narrative explodes the myth of a burgeoning Palestinian culture. When he came, the primary occupants of the land were not Arabs or Jews, but mosquitoes, which thrived in the many malarial swamps.

Twain was not the only one who recounted the bleak nature of the land at that time. In 1913, while describing the plains along the Mediterranean, the Report of the Palestine Royal Commission observed,

> The road leading from Gaza to the north was only a summer track suitable for transport by camels and carts. . . . The sanitary conditions in the village were horrible. Schools did not exist. . . . The western part, towards the sea, was almost a desert. . . . The villages in this area were few and thinly populated. Many ruins of villages were scattered over the area, as owing to the prevalence of malaria, many villages were deserted by their inhabitants.[4]

The advent of the Jewish repopulation was the beginning of a turnaround for the land.

During the administration of U.S. President Jimmy Carter, this myth of the displaced Palestinian flourished. In order to bolster this story, Joan Peters—a member of the liberal media, a White House advisor to the president and a Jew by birth— was hired to write a book promoting the Palestinian cause. As she researched, she was shocked at the reality of the situation.[5]

In *From Time Immemorial*, published in 1984, Peters presented the modern history of the land. She found that prior to the massive immigration of European Jews to the land then known as Palestine in the late nineteenth and early twentieth centuries, the land was exactly as Twain had described—barren and underpopulated. As the Jews settled, they brought trade skills, education, agricultural experience and a huge dose of work ethic. Very quickly, the landscape began to change, and the region began to prosper.

Arabs from the neighboring lands soon took notice, and many began moving to this revitalizing area to share in the fruits of Jewish ingenuity and wealth. Many of the people who call themselves Palestinians today are descendants of these recent economic immigrants.[6]

The United Nations, however, has tipped their Palestinian bias in the UN Relief and Works Agency. Through this organization, many Palestinian refugee families are receiving money equivalent to more than the average yearly salary in Lebanon. Unsurprisingly, this is causing many more Arabs to register as refugees as part of an international pseudo-social welfare program. So much of the Palestinian "problem" is simply an international con game supported by liberal international organizations and nations.

In moments of candor, even the Arabs will admit to the con. Zuheir Mohsen was a Palestinian leader of the pro-Syria as-Sa'iqa faction of the Palestinian Liberation Organization (PLO) from 1971 to 1979. In a March 1977 interview with the Dutch newspaper *Trouw*, he disclosed,

> Between Jordanians, Palestinians, Syrians, and Lebanese there are no differences. We are all part of ONE people, the Arab nation. Look, I have family members with Palestinian, Lebanese, Jordanian, and Syrian citizenship. We are ONE people. Just for political reasons we carefully underwrite our Palestinian identity, because it is of national interest for the Arabs to advocate the existence of Palestinians to balance Zionism. Yes,

the existence of a separate Palestinian identity exists only for tactical reasons. The establishment of a Palestinian state is a new tool to continue the fight against Israel and for Arab unity.[7]

The myth of the Arab nation being driven from their land is simply that—a myth. The land that is now Israel was barren and sparsely populated. The only reason it is what it is today is because of God's blessing upon the work of the Jewish people.

Deception #4: The Occupation Is the Problem

Along with the myth of the thriving Arab state is the fabrication of the Jewish occupation. The Jews did not show up out of the blue and begin kicking Arabs out of their homes.

When Jewish immigration began in the late nineteenth century, every parcel of land that these pioneers settled on already owned by an Arab was purchased fair and square. Since word got around that the settlers were backed by some big European and American financiers, the prices the owners received were typically greatly inflated.[8] Despite that truth, the enemy has many convinced that the Israelis stole the land.

Settling the land was not a matter of a group of people acting on their own initiative. The Jews had international backing throughout. In November 1917, toward the end of World War I, Arthur James Balfour, British foreign secretary at the time, wrote a letter to Lord Rothschild, a leader of the Jewish community. In this letter, he communicated his sympathy with the Jewish Zionist aspirations and made it clear that the establishment of a national home for the Jewish people would be viewed with favor by the British cabinet. This was momentous. It was the first of a series of recognitions of and permissions for a future land of Israel.

The year 1922 saw another major endorsement. The League of Nations published a "Mandate for Palestine." In this document, two regions were carved out of the greater area of this land, which at that time stretched east-west from Arabia and British Mandate Iraq to the Mediterranean and north-south from French Mandate Syria and Lebanon to Egypt. The eastern portion would be an emirate called Transjordan, governed semi-autonomously from Britain under the rule of the Hashemite family. The western portion would be Palestine, which would include a national home for the Jewish people under direct Jewish rule.

Finally, in 1948, after much political and, at times, military battling with both the British and the Arabs, Israel became an independent nation. Within eleven minutes of this event, the United States officially recognized the new nation. As soon as independence was declared, Israel was attacked by five Arab nations. These nations did not attack because of a Jewish occupation; the Israelis had been there for decades. They attacked because of Israel's very existence.

From its founding in 1964, the Palestine Liberation Organization (PLO) was the voice (and the fist) of the Palestinians. The goal of the organization, according to its name, is simply to liberate the Palestinians, but that is far from the truth. Like the Arab nations that have fought war after war with Israel, the PLO's ultimate desire, as stated in their mandate, is to destroy what they consider to be the illegitimate nation of Israel. Simply look at the map on their logo. There is no division of the land drawn in, no intention of sharing the bounty. Only when every last Jew has been pushed into the sea will these radical Arabs be satisfied.

This is why it is ridiculous when people claim that all that needs to happen for peace is for the Israelis to pull out of the land under question. The Palestinians do not want just part of the land; they want it all. Furthermore, this "solution" has been tried and was not successful. In 2005, Israel pulled out of the Gaza Strip. It was a heartbreaking process to watch. Israeli soldiers were given orders to go to Jewish homes, clear everything out and destroy the houses. Tears were shed by the homeowners and by the soldiers. Hundreds of homes that had been originally built with government approval were demolished. What did Israel receive in return for this act? Peace? Calm? Friendship? Try rockets, missiles, mortars and tunnels of terror.

There was a time, early on, when it may have been possible for peace to exist in Israel. In 1918, Hussein, the Muslim sharif of Mecca and the custodian of all holy sites, saw great potential for peace and mutual benefit between the returning Jews and the existing Arabs. Having been assured by the British authorities that the rights of the Arabs would be protected, he was very optimistic about what could happen in the land when Jews and Arabs worked side by side.[9] He expressed his optimism in an article in *Al-Qibla*, the daily newspaper of Mecca:

> The resources of the country are still virgin soil and will be developed by the Jewish immigrants. One of the most amazing things until recent times was that the Palestinian used to leave his country, wandering over the high seas in every direction. His native soil could not retain a hold on him. . . . At the same time, we have seen the Jews from foreign countries streaming to Palestine from Russia, Germany, Austria, Spain, and America. The cause of causes could not escape those who had a gift of deeper insight. They knew that the country was for its original sons [*abna'ihi-l-asliyin*], for all their differences, a sacred and beloved homeland. The return of these exiles [*jaliya*] to their homeland will prove materially and spiritually an experimental school for their brethren who are with them in the fields, factories, trades, and all things connected to the land.[10]

Hussein observed that it was good for the Jews to come back; after all, it was their land. In his wisdom, he also saw that this immigration would only benefit the Arabs living there, as well as those in the surrounding nations. But the time for that utopian scenario has passed. Sadly, there will be no peace again in the Middle East.

Deception #5: Peace in the Middle East Is Possible

Peace is a wonderful thing. We should all pray for it and strive for it in our lives. Currently, Israel is enjoying greater security than ever before. This affects every aspect of life and the very mood of the nation. But we are not fooled. There is a difference between security and peace. While we eagerly desire to have peace with the nations of the Middle East, we will not let down our guard. It is not easy to feel peaceful with your neighbors when they have sworn to wipe you off the map.

Imagine that the leaders of Mexico and Canada have pledged to destroy the United States. Every now and then, a few rockets and missiles are shot from Juarez and Nogales into Texas and Arizona. The American military naturally strikes back. But when it does, there is international outrage and a call for apologies and sanctions. Meanwhile, a steady stream of funds and arms is being passed from Canada to rebel groups within the U.S. America retaliates, destroying the border pipelines used to funnel the materials. Again, the United States is condemned by international organizations, national governments and the media. Israel finds itself in this very situation. It is no wonder that Israelis are realists about peace. If you want peace and your neighbor wants peace, there can be peace. If you want peace but your neighbor wants war, there will be war.

We just talked about the hope that Hussein, sharif of Mecca, had for Arab and Jewish cooperation and prosperity. A year later, his son, the Emir Faisal, met with Dr. Chaim Weizmann, who would later be the first president of Israel, to discuss peace. It was a very encouraging meeting. In January 1919, within the framework of the post–World War I Paris Peace Conference, Weizmann and the Emir signed a peace accord. Under the terms of the agreement, the Arabs would recognize the Balfour Declaration and encourage large-scale Jewish immigration and settlement in the land. Freedom of religion and worship in the region was set forth as a fundamental principle, and the Muslim holy sites were to remain under Muslim control. The Zionist Organization promised to look into the economic possibilities of an Arab state and committed to helping it develop its resources. Hope for a lasting friendship was great.

Less than a month later, on February 6, 1919, Faisal again appeared before the peace conference and demanded an Arab state, but he completely excluded the region called Palestine from his demands. Another great sign: Everything still seemed laid out perfectly for peace. Then intense pressure came from Arab nationalists, demanding that Faisal not abandon Palestine to the Jews. When the threats became too great, Faisal caved. He retracted the peace accord.

In place of this desire for Jewish/Arab cooperation came the first Syrian Congress, which proclaimed the Arabs' desire for a united, independent Syria, including the lands of Palestine and Lebanon. In March 1920, the Congress proclaimed Faisal the king of Greater Syria. The Europeans were not ready to let this kind of autonomy exist in the Middle East. By July, the French had driven Faisal out of Damascus, and Syria became a French mandate. The British, who had just created the state of Iraq, compensated Faisal by making him the king of this new state. Faisal's brother, Abdullah, was then made Emir of Transjordan, later becoming its king.

Any time there has been hope for peace in the Middle East, the Arab population has found a way to derail it. Hundreds of thousands have died because of their refusal to recognize the legitimacy of an Israeli homeland. It is said that Golda Meir, prime minister of Israel from 1969 to 1974, claimed, "We can forgive the Arabs for killing our children. We cannot forgive them for forcing us to kill their children. . . . We will only have peace with the Arabs when they love their children more than they hate us."[11]

There have been so many opportunities for peace. On so many occasions, a sovereign nation was offered to the Arabs alongside a Jewish homeland:

1937—The Peel Commission proposed the partition of Palestine and the creation of an Arab state. The Arabs refused.

1939—The British White Paper proposed the creation of a unitary Arab state. The Arabs refused.

1947—The UN would have created an even larger Arab state as part of its Partition Plan. The Arabs rejected it because it designated a homeland for the Jews.

1979—The Egypt-Israel peace negotiations offered the Arabs autonomy, which would almost certainly have led to full independence. The Arabs rejected the plan.

1990s—The Oslo Accords laid out a path for Palestinian independence. The Arabs derailed the process through terrorism.

2000—Israeli Prime Minister Ehud Barak offered to create a Palestinian state in all of Gaza and in 97 percent of the West Bank. The Arabs refused the plan.

2008—Israeli Prime Minister Ehud Olmert offered to withdraw from almost the entire West Bank and to partition Jerusalem on a demographic basis. The Arabs spurned that plan.

As Abba Eban, the first foreign minister of Israel, once said, "The Arabs never miss an opportunity to miss an opportunity."[12]

Desiring peace in the Middle East is chasing after the wind. The only one who will bring even a temporary halt to hostilities is the Antichrist. This brief lull he will himself soon break, according to Daniel 9:27. The possibility of lasting peace in the Middle East is a lie that Satan uses to weaken the nations and direct hostility toward Israel. Peace will only truly come when the Prince of Peace returns.

A Biblical Stand

The enemy has deceived the nations into turning their backs on Israel. As the Church becomes more secular and worldly, this deception has taken root there as well. I once heard the pastor of a huge church give a sermon over the radio. In his message, he asserted that Genesis 12:3 was not about Israel. I nearly fell off my chair.

> Now the LORD had said to Abram: "Get out of your country, from your family and from your father's house, to a land that I will show you. I will make you a great nation; I will bless you and make your name great; and you shall be a blessing. I will bless those who bless you, and I will curse him who curses you; and in you all the families of the earth shall be blessed."
>
> Genesis 12:1–3

In context, how could that be anything but a promise to Abram and his physical descendants—the people of Israel?

Churches and nations that bless Israel will be blessed by God, and those that curse Israel will suffer. The truth of the latter portion of this verse is clearly shown by Donald Grey Barnhouse, pastor for 33 years of Tenth Presbyterian Church in Philadelphia, Pennsylvania:

When the Greeks overran Palestine and desecrated the altar in the Jewish temple, they were soon conquered by Rome. When Rome killed Paul and many others, and destroyed Jerusalem under Titus, Rome soon fell. Spain was reduced to a fifth-rate nation after the Inquisition against the Jews; Poland fell after the pogroms; Hitler's Germany went down after its orgies of anti-Semitism; Britain lost her empire when she broke her faith with Israel.[13]

Throughout history, attempt after attempt has been made to destroy God's people. None have succeeded because the Lord watches over His own. Rather than destruction, we see that God takes what the enemy means for evil and uses it for good. The modern nation of Israel itself was born out of the ashes of the Holocaust. What a wonderful picture the prophet Isaiah paints of that momentous occasion on May 14, 1948: "Who has heard such a thing? Who has seen such things? Shall the earth be made to give birth in one day? Or shall a nation be born at once? For as soon as Zion was in labor, she gave birth to her children" (Isaiah 66:8).

God will judge the nations of the world because they bought into Satan's lie and, in so doing, came against Israel. The prophet Joel foresaw this time of judgment:

> For behold, in those days and at that time, when I bring back the captives of Judah and Jerusalem, I will also gather all nations, and bring them down to the Valley of Jehoshaphat; and I will enter into judgment with them there on account of My people, My heritage Israel, whom they have scattered among the nations; they have also divided up My land. They have cast lots for My people, have given a boy as payment for a harlot, and sold a girl for wine, that they may drink.
>
> Joel 3:1–3

The Church must not buy into this lie.

It is true that Israel is a secular nation. It is true that their eyes have been blinded by God to the truth of the Messiah. But that is according to the Lord's plan and His purpose and does not alter the Church's responsibility to love, pray for, care for and support God's holy nation. God will not discipline His people forever. In the meantime, the Church must stand with Israel.

7

RAPTURE:
THE GREAT MYSTERY

Up to this point, we have been focusing on the nature of biblical prophecy and Israel's role in God's plan. Now we are going to look at how the Lord's end times blueprint will take shape. As we begin this new direction, let's revisit our purpose for learning about Bible prophecy. While it can be interesting and exciting, as well as scary, God did not include the prophetic elements of Scripture just to stir our emotions. The purposes God has for giving us glimpses into the end of time are twofold: He is seeking to encourage the saints and to point to the Messiah as our hope in this world. If you are scared rather than encouraged, then you are not yet reading with accuracy. If prophecy leads you anywhere other than to Jesus Christ, then you are missing the point. Through the words of the prophets, the apostles and Christ Himself, God briefly lets us see His cards—just enough of a peek to assure us that He is playing with a winning hand.

The Great Conspiracy

One of the joys and sorrows of posting videos online is reading the many comments that people leave. Most are very encouraging and bless me greatly. Others make me shake my head and think, "You kiss your mom with that mouth?" Perusing the comments section has convinced me of one thing: The Rapture is one of the most controversial, misunderstood topics in all of theology.

Many say, "There is no such thing as the Rapture. It is the figment of a fertile imagination and faulty biblical interpretation." Some within this camp have their own alternative end times scenarios. Others simply seem to be embracing their God-given calling to be naysayers in order to balance out the yaysayers.

In the midst of all this commentary, the truth of prophecy can become lost in theories. When you add all the popular wackiness and misinformation coming from date predictors and end times preachers, theories soon become conspiracies. A prime example is the recent blood moon business. It was stunning to see all the news coverage directed at this ill-conceived idea. When the dates passed and it was shown to be another bogus notion, Christians again were seen by the world to be little different from cult members obsessed with the trajectory of the comet Hale-Bopp.

Every time a new prophecy book is published or a new prediction is made, I am inundated with this question: "Is it true?" I cannot blame anyone for asking. I would rather see people ask this question than buy into another silly scenario. But with so much disinformation out there, the truth becomes its victim.

Be encouraged: The truth is out there, and it is knowable by you and me. I have not written this book to present you with another scenario or to lay out another theory. I am sharing straight from the Bible and writing from my deepest convictions based on Scripture. When it comes to the things of God, opinions do not mean much. When Abraham was called by God, the Lord did not say, "So, Abraham, I was thinking about having you leave all you have and go to a land where you will be a stranger. What are your thoughts?" God had a plan, and He laid it out for Abraham. Man's opinion does not matter; only God's Word does.

Thus, there will be no great conspiracies woven here, no man-made date estimations given. We will deal purely with what God has revealed to us. There is trouble coming, but you will have the comfort of God's blessed hope for His people. Focusing on truth rather than opinion will ensure that you do not get caught up in the hype of the moment created by end times hucksters looking to use God to build their careers. Your peace will come from the words of the Prince of Peace. Your hope will come from the Sovereign Lord.

A Mystery Is Not a Secret

Is it really possible to understand the end times? Many believe it is not. "If God wanted us to truly know about the end times, He would have made it a lot clearer than the book of Revelation." "God wants to keep the end times a secret. After all, Matthew 24:36 says that the Father has kept the time of the Second Coming hush-hush, even from Jesus, does it not?"

But God's plan for the end times is not a secret. By definition, a secret is something hidden, something that you cannot see or feel. How illogical would it be for God to inspire the writing of so much Bible prophecy—just so that we might remain on the outside looking in? We know that God has a plan because He has told us He does. The fact that you and I have heard of the Rapture, the Tribulation, the Antichrist, the Second Coming, the Millennium and the Final Judgment means either that

God is a terrible secret-keeper or that He wants these subjects to be known.

Bible prophecy is a mystery rather than a secret. What a huge difference there is between the two! A secret is exclusionary: "I can know it, but you cannot." A mystery is inclusionary: Understanding is available to every one of us who takes the time to discover it.

Unlike a well-kept secret, a mystery does not remain hidden. Instead, it is a truth that transforms from shadow to substance. In the past, this transformation happened as God revealed more of His truth as Scripture was written. Today, this transformation typically takes place when we study and learn. We may think we understand something as it is, but then God shows more of His truth, and reality materializes out of the haze.

This process of progressive revelation is seen throughout the Bible. In the Old Testament, a promise is given that appears to be "A." Then, in the New Testament, God shows us that the promise is actually "B." In the Old Testament, at Passover the Hebrews ate the matzah and drank the wine to remember God rescuing them out of slavery to the Egyptians. In the New Testament, the Church eats the bread and drinks the cup at the Lord's table to remember Christ sacrificially rescuing us out of slavery to sin and death.

This wonderful word *mystery* is used 33 times in Scripture. Each occurrence speaks of something that can be known, whether it is the mystery of Jesus as the true Messiah (see Colossians 2:2); the mystery that Jews and Gentiles together make up the Body of Christ (see Ephesians 3:6); the mystery of the marriage-like love relationship between Christ and the Church (see Ephesians 5:31–32); or the mystery that there will be a day when the trumpet blows, and we will be changed and caught up to meet our Savior in the air (see 1 Corinthians 15:51–52;

1 Thessalonians 4:16–18). Praise the Lord that He has not kept these wonderful truths hidden!

Throughout history, trumpets were used to get people's attention. People moved when the blast was heard, whether it was giving directions on the battlefield or warning a city of imminent danger. The voice of the trumpet is also closely connected with the Rapture. As believers, we are *to be* His trumpets. God wants to blast His warning through us to make the world aware of His plans so that they, too, can be prepared for the Messiah's return.

In the book of Ezekiel, God lets His prophet feel the full gravity of his role as the warning blast for the world. The Lord finds this message so critical He gives it twice, almost word for word, first in Ezekiel 3:16–21 and then in Ezekiel 33:1–9. In these passages, God spells out the role of the watchman—the one called to warn the people of their sin and the impending judgment. Three outcomes are possible when the watchman is called into service. First, the watchman receives the word of warning from the Lord and proclaims it to the people. In response, the people repent. Yahoo, everything is great! The people are saved, and the watchman has done his job. A second scenario sees the watchman again carrying out his mandate and warning the wicked. This time they do not listen. This time it is bad news and good news: The people get the full brunt of God's wrath, but the watchman is still blessed because he did what was required of him. The third possible outcome is a lose-lose for both sides. The watchman receives the word from the Lord, but chooses not to proclaim it. As a result, the people perish, and the watchman is held accountable.

God has given us, His Church, the role of watchmen. We see the sin that the world is caught up in, and we know that judgment is coming soon. If we teach people the truth through our words and our lives, then we have fulfilled the calling that

He has given to us. What they do with the truth is between them and God.

Time is short, so we cannot afford to play around living comfortably and enjoying life. If we are to be used by God, then we must study in order to understand God's mysterious plans. Only then can we sound the alarm to those we love, as well as those God has placed in our sphere of influence.

The Mystery of the Rapture

Picture a task that you do every day; perhaps it is commuting to work or making dinner or exercising with a brisk walk. It is a day like any other day until, in the blink of an eye, it is not. You feel a change come over you—not just emotional, but physical. Then you lift off straight up into the clouds with rocket-like propulsion. You barely have time to notice that you are not the only one with these newfound aeronautic skills before you see Him: the One you have anticipated seeing your whole Christian life. You join the mass of people surrounding Him, knowing that to the Messiah you are not just another face in an ever-growing crowd. His beautiful eyes find yours, and you know more than ever how deeply He loves you. Then the journey begins again—up, up, up. You have no clue where you are headed, but there is one thing you are sure of: What you have already experienced is just the beginning of the inexpressibly wonderful eternity that your Savior, Jesus, has prepared for you.

This is the Rapture—a global, Church-wide event when Christ gathers to Himself all believers, dead and living. Paul described it this way:

> Behold, I tell you a mystery: We shall not all sleep, but we shall all be changed—in a moment, in the twinkling of an eye, at the

last trumpet. For the trumpet will sound, and the dead will be raised incorruptible, and we shall be changed.

1 Corinthians 15:51–52

In that split second, the bodies of Christians past and present will be metamorphosed, like butterflies bursting out of their cocoons. Our external shell will be transformed from this expiration-dated suit of flesh to a wonderful new creation, designed to last throughout eternity. Then we will leave the ground to meet Jesus in the air.

You might think that this dramatic event would draw quite an audience here on the earth. But look at the time frame; in "a moment, in the twinkling of an eye" this transformation will occur. Try clapping your hands together, just once. Did you do it? That is how quickly this mysterious change, this meet-the-Lord-in-the-air event will occur. On earth, it will truly be a matter of "now you see me; now you don't." Take a minute to sit back and imagine it: One moment you are going about the mundane things of life and the next you are quite literally a new person, hovering in the atmosphere with the one great God-Man you have been dying to see all your life.

If you are not eagerly anticipating your departure time, then one of three things must be true. One, you are not quite grasping the enormity of this event. Two, you have not made Jesus your Savior and your Lord. Three, you think this is a bunch of feel-good nonsense created by theologians who either are looking for an excuse to avoid the Great Tribulation or who have such poor hermeneutical skills that they have created an end times scenario that has absolutely nothing to do with reality.

If a lack of excitement is the issue, go back and reread the description of lifting off to meet your Savior face-to-face.

If the problem is that you have no hope because there is no relationship, then you can remedy that by accepting the free gift of salvation that Jesus offers to you when you trust Him to be your Savior (the One who rescues you from hell through your faith in Him) and your Lord (the One you will commit to follow throughout your life). If you find yourself in the third category, then please read on.

Some claim that the Rapture is a made-up event because it is never mentioned in the Bible. Well, I can promise you that I am not going to teach from the Koran. The Bible is the source for all truth, and the Rapture is clearly taught in the Word of God.

Harpazo is a Greek word that means to be "caught up," "snatched away" or "taken away by force." In Latin, the word *harpazo* is translated as *rapturo*, which is where we derive the word "rapture."[1]

This Greek to Latin combination is found in the Latin translation of 1 Thessalonians 4:17, as Paul describes the same event that we read about in 1 Corinthians 15. Here is the English translation: "Then we who are alive and remain shall be caught up together with them in the clouds to meet the Lord in the air. And thus we shall always be with the Lord" (1 Thessalonians 4:17). After the dead rise, the living will be caught up (*harpazo*; *rapturo*; raptured) together with them to meet Jesus.

If you are curious what *harpazo* looks like, examine other places where the word is used in a similar context. In Acts, the apostle Philip met an Ethiopian eunuch on the road. The eunuch invited Philip into his chariot, and the disciple began to explain how Jesus fulfilled the prophecies of Isaiah. Soon, the Ethiopian was looking for water in which to be baptized.

> Now when they came up out of the water, the Spirit of the Lord caught Philip away, so that the eunuch saw him no more; and he went on his way rejoicing. But Philip was found at Azotus. And passing through, he preached in all the cities till he came to Caesarea.
>
> Acts 8:39–40

One moment, Philip was with the eunuch, and the next he was gone because the Holy Spirit had "caught Philip away" (*harpazo*; *rapturo*; raptured) from one place to another. Philip had not run off. He had not said farewell or chosen another mission field to travel to. The eunuch was left standing alone, and Philip "was found" at Azotus.

Just as an aside, I love the faith of the eunuch. He was not a man who was raised in the religion of the Hebrews. In fact, he did not really have an understanding of who God was until that encounter with Philip in the chariot. Yet, when he came up out of the baptismal water and Philip suddenly disappeared, his first reaction was to praise the Lord. That is a lesson we can all take with us when strange or difficult things happen that we cannot explain.

Later, Paul had an experience that he recounted to the Corinthians, bolstering his authority in the church over the interloping "super-apostles" who were trying to lead the congregation astray. Speaking of himself in third person, he writes,

> I know a man in Christ who fourteen years ago—whether in the body I do not know, or whether out of the body I do not know, God knows—such a one was caught up to the third heaven. And I know such a man—whether in the body or out of the body I do not know, God knows—how he was caught up into Paradise and heard inexpressible words, which it is not lawful for a man to utter.
>
> 2 Corinthians 12:2–4

Two times in this passage Paul speaks of being "caught up" (*harpazo*; *rapturo*; raptured) to heaven. The Holy Spirit was the snatcher; Paul was the snatchee—and he was taken up to be in God's presence.

When I talk with people about the Rapture, there are those who say to me, "Okay, I get the mechanics of the event, but

I still have a real problem believing it." My response is, "Yes, you do have a problem." Even after reading about all the supernatural events God orchestrated in the Bible, for some, this kind of miraculous work seems like too much of a stretch in today's world.

Israel's first prime minister, David Ben-Gurion, was a very secular man. He was born in Russia and grew up in the center of the communist ideal, fitting right in with the early Zionist kibbutzim movement, which was based on that same communal philosophy. Daily prayers were not part of his routine, nor was attending synagogue every Shabbat. Even though he was as secular as the day is long, he still held regular Bible studies in his office.[2] Why? Because in Israel, you cannot avoid the divine. In an October 5, 1956, interview on CBS-TV, Ben-Gurion stated, "In Israel, in order to be a realist you must believe in miracles."[3]

Ben-Gurion's house has been preserved, and I was fascinated to discover handwritten verses from Isaiah, Jeremiah and Ezekiel under the glass cover on his desk. I was even more surprised to find a copy of Hal Lindsey's *The Late Great Planet Earth* on the bookshelf. When there is evidence of God all around you, sometimes it takes more faith *not* to believe in the miraculous.

As difficult as it can be to believe an event of this magnitude, Paul makes clear that it is going to happen:

For the Lord Himself will descend from heaven with a shout, with the voice of an archangel, and with the trumpet of God. And the dead in Christ will rise first. Then we who are alive and remain shall be caught up together with them in the clouds to meet the Lord in the air. And thus we shall always be with the Lord. Therefore comfort one another with these words.

1 Thessalonians 4:16–18

God has a great date established for us to meet Him in the air, and He has His own form of Uber to get us there.

Some may ask incredulously, "You expect us to believe that we are going to fly? Seriously?" Yes, I do. Why do we have a problem with that? Are we hung up on the law of gravity? Remember who made the law. All God needs to do is hit the "undo" button. Surely, that is not too difficult to believe. We cannot read the Bible and miss that He is a miracle worker!

I know a pastor who would take a moment with his little daughter each night after they said their prayers to stop and listen together for the trumpet of God. As sweet as that may be, the Rapture will not be announced to us this way. In Paul's description, the blare of the trumpet and the call of the archangel as the Lord begins His descent will sound in heaven only. The great sound will echo through the throne room of God to herald His departure from heaven's realm, rather than His arrival in earth's atmosphere. Even so, we must be ready for its heavenly blast. We must live our lives just as Paul did, believing that He may come in our lifetime.

Another argument leveled against the Rapture is that it does not fit the proper order of things. The writer of Hebrews says, "And as it is appointed for men to die once, but after this the judgment" (Hebrews 9:27). Everyone has a designated time when this life will end. If some people are going to finish their time on earth without death, then the only sure thing left in life will be taxes.

While living and then dying is certainly the regular order of the life cycle, departure-without-death is not without precedent. Enoch was a man who pleased God greatly; then one day the Lord snatched him away: "And Enoch walked with God; and he was not, for God took him" (Genesis 5:24). The prophet Elijah's departure was more dramatic. He and Elisha were walking on the other side of the Jordan: "Then it happened, as they continued on and talked, that suddenly a chariot of fire appeared with horses of fire, and separated the two of them; and Elijah went up by a whirlwind into heaven" (2 Kings 2:11). While rare, clearly there were individuals in Scripture who did not taste death.

"But that's just Old Testament fairy tales," some might say. "I want New Testament reality!" After Jesus' resurrection, He gathered with His disciples on the Mount of Olives. He gave them a commission to take the truth of His Gospel throughout the world: "And when he had said these things, as they were looking on, he was lifted up, and a cloud took him out of their sight" (Acts 1:9 ESV). Jesus had been dead, but He was dead no longer. The living Savior went up to heaven as a living person, and, one day, He will return as a living person. Angels confirmed this chain of events. While the disciples strained their necks, trying to see where Jesus had gone, two angels appeared next to them and said, "Men of Galilee, why do you stand gazing up into heaven? This same Jesus, who was taken up from you into heaven, will so come in like manner as you saw Him go into heaven" (Acts 1:11). He went up physically, not figuratively. He will return physically, not figuratively. While death is the traditional method of ending our earthly sojourn, it is certainly not the only one.

Calling the Ambassadors Home

The Rapture is necessary quite simply because Jesus made a promise that He needs to fulfill:

> In My Father's house are many dwelling places; if it were not so, I would have told you; for I go to prepare a place for you. If I go and prepare a place for you, I will come again and receive you to Myself, that where I am, there you may be also.
>
> John 14:2–3 NASB

Jesus promised the disciples that when He left, it would not be for good. He loved them too much to abandon His newfound

Church to a dangerous world. He would come back to receive them to Himself—and once the Church was together with their Savior, He would take them to their Father in heaven.

Some agree that Jesus is going to return and gather His Church, but then He will be taking the Church back down to earth with Him. Let us examine this supposition. True, the only real options for where the Church is heading are heaven and earth. If earth is Jesus' destination, then the event that is taking place must either be the Second Coming or the establishment of the New Jerusalem. If it is the Second Coming, then why are we going up to meet Him? Christ would need to come down to earth, but we would not need to go up to Him. He would not be receiving us—as He says He will do in John 14—so much as we would be receiving Him. Neither does Christ's return make sense in the context of the New Jerusalem because we are already with Jesus at the time it is established.

The only logical explanation is that we are taken up in order to go to heaven, where the Father is. Jesus went away at the ascension, and He will return to snatch us away using the same methodology by which He departed. Jesus will come in the clouds, He will receive us in the air and then we will leave with Him to go meet our Creator God. Let us do as Paul exhorts in 1 Thessalonians 4:18: "Therefore comfort one another with these words."

In this dangerous world, we need all the comfort that we can get. There is a war going on around us—a war we may not see, but certainly can feel. Paul writes, "For we do not wrestle against flesh and blood, but against principalities, against powers, against the rulers of the darkness of this age, against spiritual hosts of wickedness in the heavenly places" (Ephesians 6:12). These battles are taking place in the heavenly, spiritual realm. Even though they are not physical battles, they affect the physical world. That means that you and I are impacted by this spiritual war.

There are two battlefields upon which this clash is taking place. The first is in heaven. There, God has dominion through the One He has chosen to lead: Jesus Christ, who rules from His throne. The second battlefield is the world. Here, Satan has dominion by man's choice. Does this mean that Satan is superior to God on the earth? Absolutely not. God has allowed the enemy to have power here because of man's freewill decision to rebel against Him. But Satan's destiny has been sealed from the time of the very first prophecy.

Think again of Eve in the Garden admiring the one tree that she was forbidden to eat from. Along came the serpent, a physical manifestation of Satan, to plant doubt in her mind: "Did God really say?" "You can be like God." When the sins of Adam and Eve and the deceit of the devil were judged by God, He said, "And I will put enmity between you and the woman, and between your seed and her Seed; He shall bruise your head, and you shall bruise His heel" (Genesis 3:15). Satan's end was determined from the beginning, and from that point on, he has been trying his best to take as many with him as possible, to deceive as many as will listen and to cause as much chaos as he can conceive.

These are the two battlefields, but the battles fought upon them will not remain confined to these domains. The battle of heaven is now moving to the earth. In Revelation 12, the apostle John describes the vision he saw of the prelude to the heavenly war:

> Now a great sign appeared in heaven: a woman clothed with the sun, with the moon under her feet, and on her head a garland of twelve stars. Then being with child, she cried out in labor and in pain to give birth. And another sign appeared in heaven: behold, a great, fiery red dragon having seven heads and ten horns, and seven diadems on his heads. His tail drew a third of the stars of heaven and threw them to the earth. And the

dragon stood before the woman who was ready to give birth, to devour her Child as soon as it was born. She bore a male Child who was to rule all nations with a rod of iron. And her Child was caught up to God and His throne. Then the woman fled into the wilderness, where she has a place prepared by God, that they should feed her there one thousand two hundred and sixty days.

Revelation 12:1–6

The woman John describes is the nation of Israel, pregnant with the promised Messiah. Satan, the dragon, knows the ramifications of this Messiah being born and sees his chance to destroy God's plans and wreak havoc on the world. So, he waits for the child, but the Messiah consistently gives him the slip—from the moment Herod's order goes forth to kill the young boys of Bethlehem to the temptation in the wilderness to the crucifixion and resurrection. Christ accomplishes all that He was sent to do, at which time He is caught up (*harpazo*; *rapturo*; raptured) to the throne room of the Father. Israel flees to safety while the dragon goes to war. It does not go well for him:

And war broke out in heaven: Michael and his angels fought with the dragon; and the dragon and his angels fought, but they did not prevail, nor was a place found for them in heaven any longer. So the great dragon was cast out, that serpent of old, called the Devil and Satan, who deceives the whole world; he was cast to the earth, and his angels were cast out with him.

Revelation 12:7–9

The devil continues to pursue Israel while doing all he can to deceive the nations into buying his lies. Ultimately, at the end of the Tribulation, war breaks out again. Revelation 19 shows us that, as before, Satan is no match for the armies of God, and he is decisively defeated. His punishment is swift:

He laid hold of the dragon, that serpent of old, who is the Devil and Satan, and bound him for a thousand years; and he cast him into the bottomless pit, and shut him up, and set a seal on him, so that he should deceive the nations no more till the thousand years were finished. But after these things he must be released for a little while.

Revelation 20:2–3

We must recognize the warfare that is taking place if we want to discern the "why" of the Rapture.

When I was growing up, I always dreamed of being an ambassador. How incredible it would be to represent Israel to the world, hobnobbing at cocktail parties with rich and powerful people from around the globe. What a responsibility to have the leaders of Israel's government trust me to speak their words to the leaders of other nations.

That description of an ambassador's role also aptly depicts our role as Christians—although, for most, there will likely be a little less hobnobbing at cocktail parties. We represent God to the world. We speak His words and show His character through how we live. In fact, Paul uses this metaphor to portray our diplomatic function: "Now then, we are ambassadors for Christ, as though God were pleading through us: we implore you on Christ's behalf, be reconciled to God" (2 Corinthians 5:20). Note the urgency of the language Paul uses to describe this role: "As though God were pleading through us: we implore you on Christ's behalf." What a breathtaking, humbling charge.

Ambassadors are necessary communication tools between nations during good relational times and bad. When countries get along, an ambassador can work with the other nation's government to deepen friendships and negotiate mutually beneficial agreements. When times are strained between two nations, the ambassador has the more difficult, and sometimes frightening, role of making demands and leveling threats. There are also those times when negotiations break down. Governments have said all they can say to each other, and war is on the horizon. At these times, ambassadors are called home. The enemy has stopped listening, and it is no longer safe for a nation's representatives to remain in hostile territory.

There will come a time when God sees that the world is no longer listening to His ambassadors. At this moment, in the twinkling of an eye, He will call His Church back home. God's wrath is due, and the war of Revelation 19 is inevitable. A period of great tribulation will precede that horrific battle; it will be a time for the punishment of the world and preparation for Israel's conversion. What purpose would it serve for the Church to endure through the time of God's wrath if its punishment has already been paid for by Christ and its conversion has already taken place?

8

Rapture:
The Great Gathering

When I lead tours through the Holy Land, often the most difficult job is rounding everybody up. In the mornings as I load up the buses, inevitably I find at least one empty seat. When I inquire after the missing person, passengers call out, "I saw her in the gift shop," or "I saw him by the pool with a cup of coffee." You would not think that gathering together a group of adult men and women would be so difficult. It seems that the Lord has destined me to spend my days herding cats.

God is also a gatherer of people, and at the "coming of the Lord," He will have much greater success than I ever do: "Now, brethren, concerning the coming of our Lord Jesus Christ and our gathering together to Him, we ask you, not to be soon shaken in mind or troubled" (2 Thessalonians 2:1–2). There will come a time when Jesus will return to gather His Church to Himself. This is the promise of a Rapture that will take place to protect the Bride of Christ from the impending wrath of God. As Jesus tells the church of Philadelphia, "Because you have kept My command to persevere, I also will keep you from the hour of trial which shall come upon the whole world, to test those who dwell on the earth" (Revelation 3:10). The word translated "from" is the Greek word *ek*, which means "out of." This means that the Church will be kept *out of* the hour of tribulation, not *through*.

People have said to me, "Amir, you are a false teacher because you are trying so hard to make things easier for believers." I must admit, I do not quite get this argument. I do not see the logic of reading into Scripture a doctrine that is not there, just so that I can convince myself and others that we are going to have the great joy of suffering through the Tribulation. If you are determined to suffer, fear not, there will be plenty of opportunities. Christians have been promised many tribulations, just not *the* Tribulation.

The Church and Wrath Do Not Mix

The Church is not slated for the Tribulation punishment. Paul praises the Thessalonians for their commitment "to wait for His Son from heaven, whom He raised from the dead, even Jesus who delivers us from the wrath to come" (1 Thessalonians 1:10). Wrath is not for the people of God. Again, this is not without precedent. In Genesis, we read that when sin had taken over the world, God determined it would experience His wrath: "But Noah found grace in the eyes of the LORD" (Genesis 6:8). Sodom and Gomorrah had fallen so deeply into depravity that the Lord designated them for destruction. But Lot was a follower of the true God, "and while he lingered, the men took hold of his hand, his wife's hand, and the hands of his two daughters, the LORD being merciful to him, and they brought him out and set him outside the city" (Genesis 19:16). God's history shows Him rescuing His people from His wrath.

Some may ask, "What about the Tribulation saints? Surely those who become Christians during the Tribulation are going to experience Tribulation wrath." The simple answer is yes, they are. They are, however, a separate category of believers, a new people. They are not the Church because the Church is gone. Throughout all the future events spelled out in the book of Revelation, the Church is never mentioned once.[1] We will already be in heaven, experiencing the marriage ceremony with Christ (see Revelation 19:6–8). Those who are saved during the seven years of trial will endure the sorrows of the Tribulation until their lives end and God receives them into His presence.

The Rapture is a pre-Tribulation event. What would be the purpose of a Rapture that takes place at the end of the Tribulation? As far as the Church is concerned, it would accomplish nothing. Like a giant, upside-down bungee jump, the dead in Christ would rise first, followed by those who are still alive after God's wrath is poured out on the earth. They would ascend partway into the air, only to reach the end of their tether and get pulled back down to earth along with Jesus, who is returning to the Mount of Olives from which He ascended.

A well-meaning lady once approached me and said, "The Rapture is the Church going up to meet Jesus in the clouds so that we can receive Him on His way down." While that is a nice sentiment, it is illogical to me. Is the Rapture the Church's welcome wagon? Why would Jesus need us to meet Him if He is just coming down to us? Can He not come alone? Does He need some kind of moral encouragement? I believe that we will not rise to meet Him when He returns at the Second Coming because we will already be with Him. We will return to earth alongside Him.

Ultimately, the discussion boils down to the purpose of wrath. Wrath is for punishment; wrath leads to destruction. Believers do not experience the punishment of God. We will certainly experience discipline, but not punishment: "My son, do not despise the chastening of the LORD, nor detest His correction; for whom the LORD loves He corrects, just as a father the son in whom he delights" (Proverbs 3:11–12). Discipline toward correction is a very different concept with a very different purpose than the final punishment of wrath. What a joy it is to know that when we experience hardships and tribulations, God will use them for the betterment of our lives.

The Tribulation is not for the Church. If you really want to be here to experience all the horrors we read about in Revelation, then be my guest. My house is in the Valley of Armageddon, so you can have a front-row seat. I will be sure to leave the keys under the mat.

In 1 Thessalonians, Paul writes these words:

> For God did not appoint us to wrath, but to obtain salvation through our Lord Jesus Christ, who died for us, that whether we wake or sleep, we should live together with Him. Therefore comfort each other and edify one another, just as you also are doing.
>
> 1 Thessalonians 5:9–11

After bringing up the coming wrath, he says, "Therefore comfort each another." If there was a possibility that his readers would experience that wrath, how could they subsequently comfort one other? "Good news, guys, we are all going to be beheaded." "Buck up, you are about to get scorched by the sun." "Hey, all you fellow Jewish believers, pretty soon two-thirds of us are going to be slaughtered." Comfort comes when we understand what Paul wrote in verse nine: "God did not appoint us to wrath." God's wrath is coming, but the Church will not be here on earth to experience it.

What a glorious day it will be when we meet the Lord in the air! Imagine having a new body, defying the law of gravity, seeing the face of your Savior. I cannot wait to look around to see who is there with me. The church deacon who always puts money in the basket and is sure to shout "Hallelujah" loud enough to hurt God's heavenly ears may be missing from the mass of people. Meanwhile, the scruffy-looking guy from the gas station you never expected to see anywhere near a church is there smiling at you. The difference is likely that he did not fake Christ; he lived Him. We are called to live out each day the commitment we made to Christ at our conversion, praying that God will use us to help save others from the wrath that is soon to come.

What a tragedy it will be for those who are left behind because they held onto a false salvation. They played church, rather than lived as the Church. They honored God with their mouths, but their hearts were far from Him (see Matthew 15:8). Truly, not all who think they are going to be raptured are going to be raptured. That is heartbreaking.

As I have mentioned before, there is no need for us to have any fear when it comes to the end times. We can know without a doubt that when the Rapture comes, we will be with the Lord. It all comes down to what we do with Jesus. In the gospel of John, Christ makes clear the stipulation for an eternity with Him: "I am the resurrection and the life. He who believes in Me, though he may die, he shall live. And whoever lives and believes in Me shall never die" (John 11:25–26). Our Source of hope never changes. In life or in death, all rests in our Savior, Jesus Christ.

The Rapture: A Logistical Breakdown

We have considered many of the issues surrounding the Rapture, but it would be beneficial to have a step-by-step biblical breakdown. The incident will begin with Jesus Christ descending from heaven: "For the Lord Himself will descend from heaven with a shout, with the voice of an archangel, and with the trumpet of God. And the dead in Christ will rise first" (1 Thessalonians 4:16). His coming will be heralded in heaven by an archangel shouting and trumpets blaring. He is coming in order to receive us unto Himself: "And if I go and prepare a place for you, I will come again and receive you to Myself; that where I am, there you may be also" (John 14:3).

The moment Jesus arrives in the clouds, a physical transformation takes place among all believers, living and dead:

> Behold, I tell you a mystery: We shall not all sleep, but we shall all be changed—in a moment, in the twinkling of an eye, at the last trumpet. For the trumpet will sound, and the dead will be raised incorruptible, and we shall be changed.
>
> 1 Corinthians 15:51–52

In a flash, our bodies will be transformed. All our physical ailments will disappear. We will slim down without the benefit of months of Atkins dieting. We will become very fit. Our very flesh will change into a new substance—think of it as Flesh 2.0—unaffected by gravity and designed to last through eternity. Then, we launch.

The first to fly are those who are already dead. They will resurrect and rise to meet their Savior: "For this we say to you by the word of the Lord, that we who are alive and remain until the coming of the Lord will by no means precede those who are asleep" (1 Thessalonians 4:15). This resurrection will not be like that of those who were raised to life after Jesus' crucifixion. They returned to their bodies, remained alive for a time and then died again. When the dead are raised at the Rapture, it will be like the resurrection of Jesus. They will come back into a body that has been changed; it will no longer be bound by physical laws and will never deteriorate.

Now it is the turn of those believers left alive on earth: "Then we who are alive and remain shall be caught up together with them in the clouds to meet the Lord in the air. And thus we shall always be with the Lord" (1 Thessalonians 4:17). Imagine it: This is the first time that we will be able to see the entire Church from past to present. We will be saying, "Oh, there's Aunt Sue and Great-great-great-grandpa Orville! And there's my neighbor, Sheila—didn't expect to see her here—and . . . wait, where's my pastor?"

There is a promise at the end of that verse: "And thus we shall always be with the Lord." *Always* is such a wonderful word. There will never again come a time when we are separated from the manifest presence of our God—not by space, not by time, not by sin.

All of this will happen in the blink of an eye. When the earth loses its Christians, the people left behind will breathe a sigh of relief. There will be no great investigative committees or international inquiries. Christians are an impediment for evil. The Church alone stands in the way of Satan having his full way in the world.

I have a gut feeling that some of you reading this book will be alive when this happens, maybe even most of you. Paul had hope that he would experience this *harpazo*; how much more might we? Paul did not see even half the events taking place to prepare the world for the Antichrist that we have. It is said that if you go to a typical town in the United States and see Christmas lights starting to go up in all the neighborhoods, then you can be sure that Thanksgiving is right around the corner. As we will see in the chapters ahead, the lights are going up around the earth, indicating that the day is coming for Christ to return to the world that He left nearly two thousand years ago.

Let us look now at the Second Coming. A common mistake people make is to blend the Rapture and the Second Coming into one event. These are two distinct occurrences with two different purposes. At the Rapture, Christ is coming back *for* the Church. At the Second Coming, Christ is coming back *with* the Church. The prophet Zechariah writes, "And in that day His feet will stand on the Mount of Olives, which faces Jerusalem on the east. . . . Thus the LORD my God will come, and all the saints with You" (Zechariah 14:4–5). At the conclusion of the Tribulation, Jesus Christ will return to the Mount of Olives from which He departed, bringing His Bride (the believing Church) with Him.

Titus speaks of these separate events using two singular phrases. He says that the grace of God has taught us that we should be "looking for that blessed hope, and the glorious appearing of the great God and our Saviour Jesus Christ" (Titus 2:13 KJV). The world has drawn far away from God and become very anti-Christian; this downward slide will only continue. Our "blessed hope" is that a day is coming soon when our time on this earth will be over, and we will be caught up (*harpazo*; *rapturo*; raptured) to meet Christ in the air.

The "glorious appearing" of the Savior will occur just seven years later. Unlike the split-second Rapture, the Second Coming will be a process: "Behold, He is coming with clouds, and every eye will see Him, even they who pierced Him. And all the tribes of the earth will mourn because of Him" (Revelation 1:7). A period of time must pass before all are able to see Christ's descent and offer such a heartbroken and fearful response. Jesus confirmed this progression: "Then the sign of the Son of Man will appear in heaven, and then all the tribes of the earth will mourn, and they will see the Son of Man coming on the clouds of heaven with power and great glory" (Matthew 24:30). Some readers may get confused because clouds are mentioned at both events, but at the Rapture, Jesus never descends beyond cloud-level (see 1 Thessalonians 4:17).

At the event both Jesus and John refer to—the Second Coming—the response is mourning. When the Church is taken up—the Rapture—the world will be rejoicing. Mourning occurs when the world sees Jesus returning to the Mount of Olives and is confronted with their sins.

Finally, the national salvation of Israel Paul speaks of in Romans 11:26 will take place only at the glorious appearing. Of this day, Zechariah writes,

> And I will pour on the house of David and on the inhabitants of Jerusalem the Spirit of grace and supplication; then they will look on Me whom they pierced. Yes, they will mourn for Him as one mourns for his only son, and grieve for Him as one grieves for a firstborn.
>
> Zechariah 12:10

When the Messiah returns in glory, the remaining Jews will finally recognize Him for who He is, kindling a mass revival throughout the nation.

Thus, the rundown for people meeting the Lord looks like this: The dead in Christ will rise, be changed and taken up to the Savior. The living in Christ (the Church) will not die, but will be changed and taken up to the Savior. The Tribulation saints will die and be taken into the presence of God. The newly converted Jews will usher in the millennial kingdom with their Messiah. The only group not accounted for are the saints of the Old Testament. Where do they fit in?

The resurrection of the Old Testament saints will take place following the Second Coming in preparation for the Messianic Kingdom. The prophet Daniel writes of the Tribulation and the resultant resurrection:

> And there shall be a time of trouble, such as never was since there was a nation, even to that time. And at that time your people shall be delivered, every one who is found written in the

book. And many of those who sleep in the dust of the earth shall awake, some to everlasting life, some to shame and everlasting contempt.

Daniel 12:1–2

These risen saints are to be the friends of the Bridegroom at the great marriage feast. The wedding ceremony will already have taken place in heaven, but the feast will take place here on the earth—and it will be a celebration no one will want to miss: "Then he said to me, 'Write: "Blessed are those who are called to the marriage supper of the Lamb!"'" (Revelation 19:9). This will coincide with the Feast of Tabernacles, when Christ comes back and tabernacles, or resides, with His people.

Wrapping It Up

The Rapture is the promise of Christ to us. Thus, we can be assured that it will take place exactly as Scripture says it will.

The Rapture is the blessed hope of the believer. Its prospect should thrill us from top to bottom. If you find joy in the thought of staying here on this earth, then, in my view, there is something wrong in your life. If you love this world, then you are probably of this world.

The Rapture is our rescue from the evil one and from evil times. Punishment is coming for Satan and for all who follow him. God did not destine us to wrath, but to a wedding ceremony where we will experience the love of the Savior in fullness.

The Rapture is the gathering of all the saints—the first time that every Christian from the Church age will be together at one time. Imagine the celebration! Imagine the feast—all the food you want and never a worry about gaining weight. Imagine the worship in the presence of our Savior. Just imagine. . . .

Lord, come quickly.

9

THE ANTICHRIST:
THE MAN OF LAWLESSNESS

Before we move on, let us resituate ourselves. It is so easy to get caught up in the sensationalism that surrounds discussion of the end times. While there are plenty of "I didn't know that" and "Aha" moments, we cannot ever lose sight of our purpose. We are called to learn so that we can share. We are truth receivers so that we can be truth givers. Our job in these last days is to share the Word of God to a world that desperately needs to know Him. Time is short, and we have been given the momentous task of spreading the truth of the Gospel to everyone who needs the Lord's hope.

Often, when I think of the Gospel, I imagine that it is written "Gos-pills." Mankind has a sickness called sin, and this sickness will most certainly end in death. But God has given us a remedy that will cure this disease: the Gos-pills. This is not medicine that we can purchase ourselves. Instead, somebody else paid the price for this cure. When we partake of these Gos-pills, the sickness that leads to death is replaced by a faith that leads to eternal life.

Now that we have been cured, it is our responsibility to get this medication into the hands of all the terminally ill people around us. It is up to them whether they take the Gos-pills or not. Our job is simply to dispense this truth and this hope to everyone who will listen. In order to dispense the truth effectively, we need to know the truth.

The Mystery of Lawlessness

While all of God's truth is important for us to know, there are some areas that naturally pique our interest to a greater degree. The Antichrist is one of these subjects. I receive more questions about the Antichrist than any other. This is fascinating because, as the Church, we will be out of here before the Antichrist makes himself known. Rapture first, Antichrist later. Why do we care so much who this man will be?

Yet the questions pour in. "Is it Prince Charles?" "Is it Barack Obama?" "Is it Vladimir Putin or Donald Trump?" Truly, I do not know. How could I know? If I did know for sure, that would mean that he has revealed himself already, which means that I have been left behind. In that case, you cannot use my front porch for a ringside view of the great gathering at Armageddon after all: I will be using it myself.

I believe we are so intrigued because we sense that some-thing has begun, that plans are in motion. Simply looking at the world around us is enough to convince us that the mystery of lawlessness is already at work. The spirit of the Antichrist began back in the Garden of Genesis 3 and has been moving, scheming and growing ever since. As we look at our culture today, we see his rebelliousness everywhere. Sometimes this rebelliousness is overtly anti-God; other times it is simply a thread of a lie woven into a tapestry of truth. As time moves on, it will not always be easy to discern truth from falsehood. We may not know who the Antichrist will be, but we do need to know what he is all about.

This is why the emphasis should be less on the Antichrist himself and more on the lawlessness that is surrounding him. The Antichrist is not the mystery; the lawlessness is. He is only a by-product of a long line of lawlessness that began in the Garden and culminates in his rise to power. The Antichrist will not produce lawlessness; the mystery of lawlessness produces the Antichrist.

In a world that is mired in spiritual rebellion, how will it be possible to recognize this man? We know that he will be utterly consistent in his opposition to God. His desire will always be to act against the Spirit of Christ. He is a copycat to the negative—a "wanna-not-be." Just as God sent His Son to liberate and deliver us from *bondage*, ushering in peace and prosperity, so Satan will introduce deliverance from *God's Word*, establishing peace and prosperity in his own twisted way. Just as God came as a man of righteousness, so Satan will come as a man of evil. If we want to understand who the Antichrist is, we just need to know who Jesus is not. The Antichrist will make blind those who can see. He will bring death to those who are alive. He will make slaves of those who are free.

This man is the embodiment of the mystery of lawlessness. Remember, a mystery is not a secret. This mystery and its man of lawlessness are not a truth that is hidden from the eyes of the world. God has given us many clues about the part this man will play as time winds down. While the identity and timing of the Antichrist are obscured in shadows, his substance is becoming increasingly clear as the last hour draws near.

What Is the Antichrist?

"Words mean things": This maxim is particularly relevant when speaking of the Bible. There are no throwaway words in Scripture—no extra phrases to bolster the word count. One missed word or wrong definition can immediately turn truth into a lie.

Let's take a moment for a bit of grammar. There are two types of articles used in the English language: the indefinite ("a" or "an") and the definite ("the"). The indefinite article is general, while the definite is specific. Both types of articles are used in Scripture in conjunction with the word *Antichrist*.

The apostle John clearly distinguishes the difference between an antichrist and the Antichrist when he writes, "Little children, it is the last hour; and as you have heard that the Antichrist is coming, even now many antichrists have come, by which we know that it is the last hour" (1 John 2:18). While there is only one Antichrist, there are many antichrists. While the Antichrist is coming in the future, many other antichrists have come in the past and are continuing to appear. All will have the same desire to undermine the good that God is doing; the Antichrist, however, will carry out his agenda on a global scale.

How will we recognize these antichrists? It all comes down to the message. What is it that they are teaching? John writes, "Who is a liar but he who denies that Jesus is the Christ? He is antichrist who denies the Father and the Son" (1 John 2:22). Again, we see a message that is the polar opposite of Jesus' teachings.

I have been in more countries than I can count, and I have smelled a lot of smells. Some smells are wonderful: the spices of the bazaars, the flowers of Hawaii, the cool, crisp air of a Colorado morning. Others are much less appealing: the smells of war, poverty and death. The worst smell of all is one that I seem to find no matter where I am, regardless of the continent or country. It is the smell of false teaching. Somehow, I have developed a nose that can pick up heresy from a mile away. And when I search these stenches out, they always seem to center on the deity of Jesus.

The Muslims will tell you that Jesus was a great prophet. The Jews will tell you that He was a good man. Many others will say that He was a wonderfully wise teacher. But is He God? That is a step farther than any of them are willing to go.

Over the years, I have had people write to me, saying, "I used to believe in the Trinity, but now I doubt it. Jesus is the Messiah, and that is really all we need to have." This is the message that Satan has been trying to perpetuate ever since Jesus' time here on earth. Even the Jews two thousand years ago did not have a problem with Jesus being the Messiah. They laid their robes down before Him and called out, "Blessed is He who comes in the name of the LORD!" (Matthew 21:9). They were ready for Jesus to be the Messiah, but He took His message a step too far. When He was tried and crucified, it was for the blasphemous act of claiming to be God. An antichrist can be anyone who denies Jesus His deity, claiming that God is not really God.

The Antichrist is a particular person who will come at a specific time in history for an unambiguous purpose. The name *Antichrist* comes from two Greek words—*anti*, which means "opposite to, in place of" and *christos*, which means "Christ." The Antichrist is someone who is opposite to Christ or who acts in the place of Christ. As we have already seen in this chapter, his name fits him perfectly.

If God is the Father of Jesus Christ, then it makes sense that Satan is the father of the Antichrist. If we want to know the character of Jesus, we look to the Father. Likewise, if we want to know what the Antichrist is like, we should look to the father of lies. Satan is obsessed with wanting to be like God. His first earthly success came when he promised Eve the same lie that he had bought into: "You will be like God" (Genesis 3:5). Satan was attempting to convince the woman of that which was in his own heart. Isaiah puts these words in the mouth of the evil one: "I will ascend above the heights of the clouds, I will be like the Most High" (Isaiah 14:14). The whole mystery of lawlessness began with Satan's own ambitious heart, spread to the Garden and then, like a spiritual version of the Black Death, infected the rest of the earth.

What is shocking is that there is an established movement of those who say that this spread is a good thing. They claim that God is the problem and Lucifer is really the good guy. Proudly, they represent Satan and choose him over the blessed hope. Sadly, the day will come when they will realize the folly of their choice.

When Is the Antichrist Coming?

In the time of Paul, there was a lot of deception and bad information floating around regarding times and seasons. Many thought that Emperor Nero was the Antichrist due to his atrocities and some number play connecting his name with the number 666. That particular deception still holds true among many schools of thought.

Concerned about the false theories regarding the end times that were circulating through the fledgling churches, Paul wrote to the church at Thessalonica:

> Now, brethren, concerning the coming of our Lord Jesus Christ and our gathering together to Him, we ask you, not to be soon shaken in mind or troubled, either by spirit or by word or by letter, as if from us, as though the day of Christ had come. Let no one deceive you by any means; for that Day will not come unless the falling away comes first, and the man of sin is revealed, the son of perdition, who opposes and exalts himself

above all that is called God or that is worshiped, so that he sits as God in the temple of God, showing himself that he is God.

2 Thessalonians 2:1–4

According to Paul, people are going to say that the day of Christ has already come; furthermore, they are going to claim that they speak these words on His behalf. Do not believe it. Others will proclaim that they are preaching words the Holy Spirit gave to them, but these words cannot be true.

Paul makes it clear that the Day of the Lord is still coming. God is bringing His judgment upon the world, but two things must happen before this can take place. First, there will be a great apostasy from the truth of God. Second, the Antichrist must come. Neither of these events can be shown to have taken place. Yet the day will come when this man will exalt himself as if he is God, and he will lead a willing people to worship him. He will go to the Temple and deceive people into believing he is deity.

If he is going to be worshiped at the Temple, what is the underlying assumption? The assumption is that there is a Temple in which he can be worshiped. I come from Israel. I have been in Jerusalem more times than I can possibly count. I can tell you with absolute certainty: There is no Temple in Jerusalem. Thus, the events of 2 Thessalonians 2 must take place in the future.

The idea of a Temple in Jerusalem casts the whole timeline into doubt for many. Some believe that it is impossible ever to have the Temple rebuilt. It is inconceivable that the Muslims would allow it. The Temple Mount is already the home of the Dome of the Rock, the Al-Aqsa Mosque and the Dome of the Chain—three of the most revered sites in Islam. It would be tough to squeeze in a Jewish temple up there.

But this is the power of the deception of the Antichrist. We do not know how he will do it. Paul, however, makes it clear that he will. Once permission is given for the building of the Temple, it will go up quickly. Already there is a Temple Institute in Jerusalem. All of the worship vessels are prepared, and the blueprints are drawn up. They are only waiting on the go-ahead to build. What they do not understand is that the man who finally gains this permission only intends the Temple to be rebuilt so that he can be worshiped in it. I suspect that the Jews are going to be fairly angry when they figure that out.

The Antichrist is not a friend of the Jews. This is a truth that the Jews will learn the hard way. If you remember, Revelation 12 gives us a picture of the war in heaven. The dragon will show his face and persecute the woman—Israel—who will give birth to Christ. Satan desperately wants to destroy the nation of Israel because he knows that their role in God's plan is not yet done.

Jesus said to the city of Jerusalem, "For I say to you, you shall see Me no more till you say, 'Blessed is He who comes in the name of the LORD'" (Matthew 23:39). In order for Jesus to return at the Second Coming, the Jews must be in their city, entreating Him to come back. Thus, all that is needed to prevent Jesus' return is to wipe out the Jews. No matter how hard Satan has worked to destroy God's chosen people, however, they just keep coming back.

Israel is a survivor. Despite dispersions, crusades, inquisitions, pogroms and the Holocaust, Satan cannot find a permanent way to get rid of this threat to his existence. He never will figure it out because God is on their side. The Lord is there with His people.

Satan tries to destroy Israel, and Satan fails. Satan fights God, and Satan loses. He lost the war in heaven, and he is about to lose the war on earth. How do I know this? It is all in the Bible.

Why Is the Antichrist Coming?

In order to gain a conviction in a court case, a district attorney must show motive. Why did the perpetrator do what he did?

This "why" question must also be put to the Antichrist. We have addressed when he will come, and we have seen some of what he will do when he shows himself. But before we move on, we must look into his motivation.

We do not have to search far. Returning to 2 Thessalonians, we see that Paul answers this all-important question:

> The coming of the lawless one is according to the working of Satan, with all power, signs, and lying wonders, and with all unrighteous deception among those who perish, because they did not receive the love of the truth, that they might be saved. And for this reason God will send them strong delusion, that they should believe the lie, that they all may be condemned who did not believe the truth but had pleasure in unrighteousness.
>
> 2 Thessalonians 2:9–12

The Antichrist is coming to step into the void left by the rejection of Christ. The people of this world turned their backs on the truth of God and accepted the falsehoods of the liar and deceiver. John puts it this way: "He was in the world, and the world was made through Him, and the world did not know Him. He came to His own, and His own did not receive Him" (John 1:10–11). The Antichrist is coming to be received by those who refused to receive Christ.

Because the world will choose the Antichrist over the Christ, God will send the people a strong delusion so that they become entrenched in this lie. Just look around at how rooted our culture is in unrighteousness. People seem to revel in anything that is opposite of God. The deceptions of the father of lies have tainted the worldviews of mankind, paving the way for the one who is anti-Christ in all respects.

Earlier, we discussed the two tracks of deception that Satan will take with the world. Most of our time was spent with the second track—the deception of the nations. However, it is the first of the two tracks—the deception of the world—which will usher in the time of the Antichrist. History has proven that the deceiver understands humanity thoroughly. He knows which of our desires to tap into to gain maximum effect. Already, we can see his success in exploiting our greatest longings.

The first desire he taps into is the world's desire for prosperity. People want money, comfort, expensive toys and pretty baubles. A growing sense of altruism causes people to want and expect these things not only for themselves but for everyone. This seems to be a major goal for many world governments and world leaders, including the previous American president. As a result, through alliances, trade deals and climate change protocols, the world is moving toward a system that will secure prosperity for all.

Many twentieth-century monetary systems throw a wrench into the workings of global prosperity. Someone is always speculating with currencies—assigning greater value to one while devaluing another. Currently, the U.S. dollar is the standard for most of the world's financial dealings. If the global market decided to stop using the dollar, then the dollar would collapse. There is too much risk in the old system. The best option for the rich to stay rich and the poor to move up the financial ladder is to create a one world economy based on one currency with one world reserve.

The United States will readily join in, especially as its debt multiplies and the tenuousness of the dollar grows. As of now, much of the country's economic system is controlled by the Federal Reserve. Most people do not realize that this is a privately owned bank. Through the Federal Reserve, five wealthy families are pulling the strings of the nation's economy—a huge amount of power in a few relatively anonymous hands. There will be a sigh of relief from many when the financial decisions of the nation are controlled by a seemingly more compassionate and globally minded international body.

What began in Europe will spread throughout the globe—many nations uniting under one economy and one currency. The goal will ultimately be a cashless system: no coin, no paper, no fraud, no hassle. It will be an easy sell in the name of security. Already cash is being used less and less. Most economic activity now takes place digitally by card or online. I have a friend who rarely carries any cash at all; it is just not necessary anymore. The desire for convenience pushes us toward a cashless society, and the desire for security pushes us toward unity.

The people's desire for unity is, in fact, the second human desire that Satan takes advantage of. Out of this longing a one world government will rise, though it may seem like an impossible task. How could anyone possibly bring *e pluribus unum* ("out of many, one") to this world with its many peoples and cultures? There are so many rivalries, so much bloody water that has flowed under nationalist bridges. Some great, unifying cause would need to supersede all the factions and bitterness.

This cause exists today and has already started breaking down borders and uniting governments. In the last two decades, more than 190 countries have given up part of their sovereignty to a governing treaty called the Kyoto Protocol, originally adopted in 1997 in Kyoto, Japan, with the goal of saving the earth from global warming.[1]

According to proponents of global warming, the earth is on a downward slide toward destruction, man-made carbon emissions being the greatest culprit. Because this is not a localized climate emergency, allowing each nation to determine its own course of action is inadequate. A global problem demands global oversight.

This doomsday ideology has permeated every aspect of our world. In 2015, President Barack Obama declared climate change to be the single greatest threat to future generations.[2] Economies suffer due to excessive regulations and denials of new energy projects all in the name of saving the world.

A smoldering panic at melting polar ice caps and diminishing food supplies has saturated a great many cultures. The science that has led to these conclusions is no longer questioned. Like the theory of evolution, the theory of climate change is now accepted as scientific law.

The reach of global warming is even extending into religion. A growing trend of evangelical environmentalism is shifting Christians' focus from saving souls to saving the planet. In the Catholic Church, Pope Francis has taken on climate change as a key component in his spiritual platform. In an encyclical released in June 2015, Francis called for the creation of a new global political authority that would tackle the challenge of reducing pollution.[3] Then, in September 2016, the Pope pronounced that committing "a crime against the natural world is a sin against ourselves and a sin against God."[4] Who will determine what is a "crime against the natural world"? I suppose that will be the new global climate authority that Pope Francis has proposed.

While there might be a temporary reprieve from a unifying global climate power due to recent elections in the United States and Europe, this reprieve will be short-lived. The belief that we are rapidly destroying our earth has become a permanent element of a universal worldview and has been entrenched in the hearts and minds of our upcoming generations.

A longing for global peace is the third desire that the deceiver effectively utilizes. With daily reports of terrorism and the expanding threat of nuclear weapons, it is no wonder folks are crying for everyone to please get along. The center point of this peace focus is the Middle East. There is a belief that if we can somehow achieve peace in that region of the globe, then that good neighborliness will spread to the rest of the world. So, when the Antichrist actually achieves peace in the Middle Eastern hot zone, the world will rise up and call him blessed.

The prophet Daniel writes,

> Then he shall confirm a covenant with many for one week; but in the middle of the week he shall bring an end to sacrifice and offering. And on the wing of abominations shall be one who makes desolate, even until the consummation, which is determined, is poured out on the desolate.
>
> Daniel 9:27

The period of this peace accord is seven years (one week); this time will be so appealing that the battle-weary world will choose to follow and worship the Antichrist. What the people do not know is that when half of the week has passed (three-and-a-half years), he will break his own covenant.

A temporary peace broken by the peacemaker himself is characteristic of the Antichrist because it is completely opposite from that which God brings. When the Lord brings peace, it is always a complete peace: "Now may the Lord of peace Himself give you peace always in every way" (2 Thessalonians 3:16). People would have to be out of their minds to choose the peace of Satan over the peace of God—but people are out of their minds.

A number of years ago, I was sent to Germany to question a defector from the Iranian army. He gave up a lot of information about the Iranian Revolutionary Guard, including who it was made up of and how they operated. But it was nothing new—information I already had. Then he said something that made me sit up and take notice. I was shocked at what I heard, but then I was shocked that I was shocked, because his words actually answered many questions. In the Iranian army, the soldiers, from the highest commander to the least of the grunts, are all on drugs—and not just alcohol or marijuana. The drugs they use are heavy duty. This is why a military system based on blind, mindless obedience actually works; the soldiers are not able to think.

Our world is much the same. Drugs are being promoted as not just legal but beneficial. Nearly eighty percent of the world's opioid pain medications are consumed in the United States, and the legalization of recreational marijuana has recently expanded from Colorado to more and more states. What once was considered taboo, public companies now produce, and our laws proclaim it as "good."

Whether it is because they are out of their minds or because the prevalence of drug use has destroyed their thinking processes, people will choose Satan's peace over God's peace. The world is looking for a hero, not a suffering Messiah. Christ was supposed to save the world; instead, He was found walking to the cross. The Antichrist will show himself to be the champion that all are looking for: "And I saw one of his heads as if it had been mortally wounded, and his deadly wound was healed. And all the world marveled and followed the beast" (Revelation 13:3).

Satan knows the heart of mankind. He knows what motivates and excites people. That knowledge allows him to manipulate humanity into buying his lies, heart and soul.

Where Will the Antichrist Come From?

This is the final question that I hear most often: Where will the Antichrist come from? That is a tricky question that requires a look at biblical evidence, history and world culture. There are those who say that the Antichrist will be a Muslim. Islam is spreading and permeating many nations, and its power seems to be growing greater and greater. It used to be that this spread was contained to the Middle East, southern Asia and northern Africa, but now Europe and the United States are dealing with their own issues of expanding Islamization.

A Muslim Antichrist is an absolute impossibility, however. Show me one Jew who would choose a Muslim to be his Messiah. You could not find a Jew who would allow a Muslim to be his prime minister, let alone the Chosen One they have been praying for the last two-thousand-plus years. Also, show me one Muslim who would allow the Jews to build the Temple on the Temple Mount. The Koran forbids Muslims from making a peace treaty with the Jews. The idea of giving up some of their holy ground for a Jewish Temple without being tricked or deceived in some remarkable way is inconceivable.

What is going to change that will allow the building of the Temple? By the time the Antichrist reveals himself, Islam will be much less a global factor than it is today. Already, this belief system is in its last days, primarily because it is so violent. Soon, the radicals will become so extreme in their actions that the more moderate Muslims will be forced to disavow them. Islam will become mainstream in practice and in culture. Rather than emphasizing their distinctiveness, particularly through their adherence to *sharia* law, Muslims will assimilate and integrate into European culture, accepting the Vatican's new "be good" philosophy. There will be little need for a compromise of their theology because European theology is a "kumbaya" mush.

The Antichrist will certainly not come out of the Middle East. To discover his true origins, we need to go back in history. The great King Nebuchadnezzar built the Empire of Babylon, but he was not the first to build a civilization in that region. *Babylon* in Hebrew is "Babel."

Genesis 11 tells us the first inhabitants of this land ran into a problem with God. They wanted to build a tower that reached into heaven. This sounded like a good idea to them because, in their minds, if you make it to heaven, then you become God. They simply forgot that you cannot put one over on God. He knew exactly what they were doing, so He confused their language and sent them out. The area became known as Babel—an onomatopoeic word that is based on the sound of a foreign language to one's ears. From the beginning, Babylon was a place of confusion and of a longing to be like God.

Nebuchadnezzar fit perfectly into this mold. As he was admiring the kingdom from his rooftop one day, he began praising himself for all that he had done, putting himself in the role of god over his empire. The Lord stepped in and said,

> The kingdom has departed from you! And they shall drive you from men, and your dwelling shall be with the beasts of the field. They shall make you eat grass like oxen; and seven times shall pass over you, until you know that the Most High rules in the kingdom of men, and gives it to whomever He chooses.
>
> Daniel 4:31–32

Immediately, Nebuchadnezzar's senses left him, and his mind was filled with confusion until the time when he looked to heaven and gave God the glory for all that he had.

What better place from which to see the Antichrist rise than Babylon? "Wait a second, Amir, are you saying that the Antichrist will be an Iraqi? Isn't that where Babylon is? You just said he will not come out of the Middle East!" No, I am not saying the Antichrist will be from Iraq.

In the sixth century BC, the Babylonian Empire was destroyed by the Medes and Persians in Babylon. The Persians ruled until the fourth century BC, when their empire was destroyed by the Greeks, under the leadership of Alexander the Great, in Babylon—the city where Alexander died ten years later in 323 BC. The Greek Empire was the dominant power until it was destroyed by the Romans in Babylon. The Roman Empire was vast and powerful and ruled for centuries, but even it was eventually destroyed, except not in Babylon. The Germanic tribes, the Alemanni, were the ones who brought down the empire by causing it to spread out and disintegrate (again, not in Babylon, but in Europe). This shift from the Middle East to Europe is significant.

Daniel 7 records a dream that the prophet had one night as he was lying in his bed. Out of the sea came four beasts. The first had the appearance of a lion with an eagle's wings. The second looked like a bear. The third was a four-headed, four-winged, leopard-looking creature. Then Daniel describes the fourth beast:

> After this I saw in the night visions, and behold, a fourth beast, dreadful and terrible, exceedingly strong. It had huge iron teeth; it was devouring, breaking in pieces, and trampling the residue with its feet. It was different from all the beasts that were before it, and it had ten horns. I was considering the horns, and there was another horn, a little one, coming up among them, before whom three of the first horns were plucked out by the roots. And there, in this horn, were eyes like the eyes of a man, and a mouth speaking pompous words.
>
> Daniel 7:7–8

This final beast describes the Roman Empire. Out of the head of this beast grows ten horns with three "plucked out by the roots." Western Europe is the only area that has had ten tribes with three that no longer exist: the Visigoths (Spain), Anglo-Saxons (England), Franks (France), Alemanni (Germany), Burgundians (Switzerland), Lombards (Italy), Suevi (Portugal), Heruli (rooted up), Ostrogoths (rooted up) and Vandals (rooted up). Ten tribes: Seven still exist, and three are gone. What about that small horn that will come up among them, "speaking pompous words"? This is the Antichrist. He is coming, and it seems the world is paving the way for his arrival.

10

THE ANTICHRIST: ROLLING OUT THE RED CARPET

Imagine that you have been warned that you will die by falling off the observation deck of the Empire State Building on March 26, 2024. The most logical response would be to make sure you were somewhere else entirely on that day. If you decided to ignore the warning and take in a skyscraper view of New York City that day, then you would only have yourself to blame as you saw your image, reflected in office windows, hurtle past.

God has alerted the world of the coming man of lawlessness. He has clued us in as to his identity and origin. Furthermore, the Bible overflows with warnings against abandoning the Lord, plunging into sensuality, neglecting the helpless or relishing unrighteousness. When we look around, however, that is often all we see. The world is ignoring God's warnings, ascending step-by-step to the top of the skyscraper to take its plunge. The continent leading the march toward the end is Europe.

Europe: Modern-Day Babylon

To see Babylon in Europe today is not difficult. All one needs to do is to look. First, Babylon is apparent in the symbols of Europe. The European flag has a rich blue background upon which are placed twelve stars in a circle. This pattern of twelve stars is known as the Queen of Heaven, a title of great historical significance.[1]

To examine that significance, let us go back to Genesis and the origin of Babylon. Nimrod, the great-grandson of Noah, was its builder. He was called, according to Genesis 10:9, a "mighty hunter before the LORD." The title given by the Babylonians to the mother of this great man was the "Queen of Heaven." Later, Greek mythology made Nimrod a great warrior and the builder of the Tower of Babel. This tower became a satanic symbol of rebellion against God. It stood for humanity's attempts either to prove that there is no God or to replace Him. Who else in this world works to prove to humanity that there is no God and that He is replaceable?

As mentioned earlier, God destroyed the tower, but the city continued to be seen as a symbol of sin and rebellion against God. How interesting it is that when God exiled His people from their land due to their rebellion, He sent them to Babylon—the city of rebellion! This city of insurrection against the Lord has become a symbol that the leaders of Europe have adopted for themselves.

In 1563, Pieter Bruegel the Elder painted his vision of what the Tower of Babel may have looked like. This remarkable work shows an unfinished tower with scaffolding set up at various points around it, just barely reaching above cloud level. Currently, it may be found hanging in Vienna at the Kunsthistorisches Museum. If you were to take Bruegel the Elder's *Tower of Babel* and place it up against a picture of the EU Parliament building in Strasbourg, France, you would find remarkable similarities. These parallels are intentional. This multimillion-dollar complex that was completed in 2000 was designed after the sixteenth-century painting and stands as a symbol of the pride that man takes in his rebellion against God.[2]

"Oh, Amir, shame on you! You have such imagination! It does not even look the same." Sure it does. Substitute glass and steel for stone, and you will find a surprisingly close replica. Need a little more proof? In a poster produced by the European Union, what do you find? A replica of Bruegel the Elder's *Tower of Babel* with the caption "Europe: Many Tongues, One Voice."[3] On another poster the EU released entitled EUROPE-4ALL, we see a star made up of the symbols of all the world's belief systems—a cross, a crescent moon, a star of David, yin/yang, hammer and sickle and many others, along with the caption "We can all share the same star."[4]

This is part of the push toward one religion. Break down the barriers between beliefs and focus on what brings us all together.

"Oh, Amir, you're really stretching it!" Am I? There is a sculpture by Léon de Pas outside the EU Council building in Brussels called *Europe en avant*, which is French for "Europe forward."[5]

This work is based on the Greek mythological story of the rape of Europa—Europa being the basis for the name Europe. In this story, Zeus disguised himself as a white bull in order to seduce the princess, Europa, who was out gathering flowers. When she approached the bull and climbed on its back, the bull seized the occasion to run away with her and eventually rape her. After her eventual death, she received divine honors as the "Queen of Heaven."

This is the woman John saw when he wrote Revelation 17. In it he described a very wealthy continent:

So he carried me away in the Spirit into the wilderness. And I saw a woman sitting on a scarlet beast which was full of names of blasphemy, having seven heads and ten horns. The woman was arrayed in purple and scarlet, and adorned with gold and precious stones and pearls, having in her hand a golden cup full of abominations and the filthiness of her fornication. And on her forehead a name was written:

MYSTERY, BABYLON THE GREAT, THE MOTHER OF HARLOTS AND OF THE ABOMINATIONS OF THE EARTH.

Revelation 17:3–5

John saw the woman that the European Union has taken as their symbol, a symbol based on Greek mythology.[6] The EU is not intentionally trying to become what John described; they are just being who they are. This woman riding the beast continues to be a prevalent symbol in modern Europe. It was seen in 1948 on a German five-mark note.[7] In 1979, it appeared in a painting on the Berlin wall. In 1984, she was placed on a British stamp commemorating the second European parliamentary elections. In 1992, Europa riding the bull was minted on a German EQ coin (the EQ was the predecessor to the euro). And today, you can find this symbolism on a painting in the airport lounge in Brussels, on a German telephone card and on the back of the new two-euro coin in Greece. Just recently, the European Central Bank released the Europa series of euro banknotes that feature an image of the goddess as a key element of the currency's security features.[8] The Queen of Heaven is alive and well in Europe.

Another evidence of Babylon in Europe is in its desire to import Babylon to continental soil. Many are familiar with the old reels of Adolf Hitler giving impassioned speeches to thousands of German soldiers lined up in tight formation across a vast field in Nuremberg called Das Zeppelinfeld. Behind him was an enormous cement grandstand, new in construction but classical in appearance. This grandstand, designed by Hitler's architect,

Albert Speer, is modeled after the Altar of Zeus, also known as the Seat of Satan. For Speer to design such a spectacular edifice, one would think he had traveled somewhere distant to study the ancient ruins, seeking for a way to re-create this ancient place of pagan worship. Yet that is far from the truth.

Pergamum was a beautiful city of the Roman Empire. Located in what is now southern Turkey, it was a rich and intelligent metropolis, a city of inventors and innovators. It once housed a library so vast that Mark Antony gifted Cleopatra the entire library of Pergamum in order to show the depth of his love for her. It was a wonderful city, yet utterly evil at the same time.

Along with all the wealth and learning, Pergamum was also home to the Altar of Zeus. Horrific things took place on that altar—both of worship and violence. In one occurrence, an early church leader was arrested. When he would not recant his faith, he was placed inside a large bronze bull used for holding sacrifices and roasted alive.[9] This man's name was Antipas, and Jesus remembered him when He said about the church in Pergamum,

> I know your works, and where you dwell, where Satan's throne is. And you hold fast to My name, and did not deny My faith even in the days in which Antipas was My faithful martyr, who was killed among you, where Satan dwells.
>
> Revelation 2:13

When Albert Speer designed the grandstand of Das Zeppelinfeld after this Altar of Zeus, he did not need to take a trip down to southern Turkey; he only needed to go across the city of Berlin to Museum Island.[10] The largest of the museums on this island is the Pergamon Museum, a museum which now houses the Altar of Zeus—the real deal, not a replica. The actual altar was dismantled, moved to Berlin and reconstructed in 1930. Babylon and its worship of Satan are now in Europe.

Hitler was not a Christian, as many now try to claim through revisionist history. He was a follower of Satan. The Seat of Satan was what he chose for his grandstand. Satan came to Germany; then Germany tried to accomplish what the evil one has been trying to do from the beginning—kill the Jews.

"Amir, you are stretching it! Babylon to Berlin? Come on!" Did you know that in 586 BC, when the Jews were led into Babylonian exile, they entered the city through the Ishtar Gate—a beautiful brick archway, painted blue and decorated with six gold animals? Do you know where you will find this gate today? In Berlin, at the same Pergamon Museum where the Altar of Zeus is located. Babylon is being imported to Europe.

Finally, Europe is emulating Babylon in its desire, like Babel, to unify under one anti-God banner. One of the most powerful organizations ever developed was born out of the Crusades. When Jerusalem was conquered by Europe, pilgrims began to flow to the Holy Land. But the journey was treacherous and grueling with bandits waiting in ambush along the way. To protect these pilgrims, the Order of the Knights Templar was created, eventually becoming an elite fighting force.

When the knights' great strength was combined with a lack of structural oversight and accountability, it was not long before they lost their original, altruistic purpose. Satan's voice whispered, "Money is the way to take over the world." And the knights listened.

If you have ever written a check, you understand that the check is not money. The check simply represents money. This integral part of our modern banking system was developed by the Knights Templar.[11] They saw that somewhere around ten percent of the Crusaders actually made it all the way to Israel. For these Crusaders, leaving all their money back home was dangerous; perhaps your neighbors would hear a rumor of your death and take it. It was also dangerous to bring your money along; you could be robbed. So, the Knights opened two banking offices: one in Europe and one in the Holy Land. They said, "Leave your money with us, and we will issue you a check. Take the check with you, and, when you arrive in the Holy Land, simply present that check, and we will give you all your money." This was an absolutely brilliant business move. If only ten percent of the Crusaders made it to the Holy Land, then ninety percent did not. Who kept the money of those lost along the way? The Knights Templar did. In today's terms, this amount equaled billions of dollars. Think of it this way: If you have so much money that even the Pope is afraid of you, then you have some serious cash.

The absolute power of the Templars corrupted them absolutely. They became a small group of people with an enormous amount of influence throughout all of Europe who vowed to use their banking system to oppose God. When the rumors of their corruption became too great, King Philip IV of France spearheaded a series of inquisitions. Charges brought against the Templars included heresy, desecration of the cross, and idol worship (specifically, the worship of Satan in the form of Baphomet—a human figure with the head of a goat). In March 1312, Pope Clement V issued a papal bull disbanding the order, and they subsequently went underground.[12]

As an aside, in 2015, a nine-foot-tall, 1.5-ton sculpture of Baphomet was placed in a building in Detroit. This statue depicts Satan sitting on his throne with a young boy and young girl on either side looking up longingly at him. At the event that revealed this heinous effigy, a crowd danced and partied, while cries of "Hail, Satan!" filled the room.[13] Yes, the devil is alive and well in the United States, too.

The next time we see a move to European unification is in the eighteenth century during the Enlightenment era. It is at this time that a group known as the Bavarian Illuminati begins to surface. The term *illuminati* is simply a fancier way of saying "the enlightened ones"—those who have received or discovered special knowledge.

The growth of this new group of one world unifiers began with an influential Jew. Keep in mind that some Jews are not really Jews. Rather than being part of God's chosen people, they actually belong to the synagogue of Satan, serving as antichrists.

Adam Weishaupt was born a Bavarian Jew but was educated by Jesuits who forced him to convert to Catholicism. A professor of natural and canon law at Ingolstadt, he eventually began to follow esoteric teachings. It was not, Weishaupt argued, that he was "against religion itself, but rather the way in which it was practiced and imposed"; his new society "offered freedom 'from all religious prejudices.'"[14] In May 1776, a group of five men, Weishaupt's own students, met "to found the order in a forest near Ingolstadt"; they were the first Illuminati. As the secret society grew, prominent men joined the ranks, including Baron Adolph von Knigge, who helped solidify the society's association with Freemasonry, and Mayer Amschel Rothschild, who, as a wealthy banker, "provided funding."[15] It was out of these meetings that the Bavarian Illuminati was born—this name being taken from a 1640 German occult society.

By 1778, the Illuminati "began to make contact with various Masonic lodges, where, under the impulse of [Baron von Knigge], one of their chief converts, they often managed to gain a commanding position."[16] This connection with the Masons allowed for the rapid extension of the Illuminati's influence. Eventually, in its heyday, the Bavarian Illuminati achieved an impressive spread "from Italy to Denmark and from Warsaw to Paris."[17] As the illuminated ones, the "light bearers," the Illuminati were determined to unify the world and then take it over. In 1785, however, the society was "banned by an edict of the Bavarian government."[18] From that time on, any further spread occurred as an underground movement; in the meantime, the important association between the Illuminati and Freemasonry, another secret society, was preserved.

The Freemasons began as a guild of builders in the fourteenth century. Originally, they functioned somewhat similarly to a modern union—maintaining building standards and ensuring the quality of the workers. By the late 1700s, fewer castles were being built, and no one was erecting giant cathedrals anymore. During this lull, the Masons lost their purpose, and many builders lost their jobs.[19]

Faced with the option of reinventing themselves or dissolving, the Freemasons chose to morph from a guild to a belief system. This is when the Illuminati infiltrated their ranks. Soon, the Masons became much more secretive and began printing various materials based on occult principles. An organization that began innocently enough became thoroughly subverted by the light of Lucifer.

It is likely that many of you know men and women involved in Freemasonry. They may be your relatives, your neighbor or a deacon in your church. "Are all of them devil-worshipers?" you might ask. I believe that many, possibly even a majority, of those involved in Freemasonry have no idea what it is really all about. To them, it is a social club or a networking society. They have never taken the time to dig deep and learn. This does not excuse their being part of this occult group. Everyone, particularly those who claim the name of Christ, should separate themselves from Freemasons immediately.

The deceiver began in the Garden of Eden, spread his deception through history and found a new home for it in Europe. The Europeans, through Freemasonry, then exported his lies to America. The goal of this deception was to unite all people, not under the banner of the cross, but under the deceits of the evil one. This unifying move toward a one world government took hold in the early twentieth century and has been growing ever since.

- The Pan-European Movement (1923–26): In 1923, the Austrian Count Richard Nikolaus Graf Coudenhove-Kalergi founded this movement based on the goal of uniting all Europeans under a European nation built on a homogenized European culture. "In 1926, he managed to bring together numerous diverse political figures in the First Pan-European Congress, held in Vienna."[20]
- The Schuman Declaration (1950): On May 9, 1950, French foreign minister Robert Schuman "propos[ed] that France and Germany and any other European country wishing to join them pool their [c]oal and [s]teel resources." The goal was the gradual integration of European economic resources and a move away from the hostilities surrounding the wars of the first half of the century.[21]
- The Treaty of Paris (1951): Originally called the Treaty establishing the European Coal and Steel Community (ECSC), this pact united France, West Germany, Italy and the Benelux countries (Belgium, the Netherlands, and Luxembourg) together into an international community. Systematization of the free movement of coal and steel and open access to sources of production were the goals of this international consortium. A High Authority was instituted and tasked with the supervision of the market, the competition rules, and pricing. The economic cooperation that exists within the EU finds its foundation in this treaty.[22]
- The Treaty of Rome (1957): Officially, the Treaty establishing the European Economic Community (EEC Treaty), this gathering merged the markets of the six European Coal and Steel Community (ECSC) nations, laying the

foundation for the future European Union. The location of this event was symbolic, pointing to the revival of the Roman Empire.[23]

- The Single European Act (1987): Signed in Luxembourg and The Hague, this treaty modified the initial treaties of the European Communities. It set the goal of establishing a single European market by December 31, 1992.[24]

- The Treaty of Maastricht (1992): Much changed with this agreement. Also known as the Treaty of the European Union (TEU), this pact shifted the ultimate goal of the European community from economic cooperation to political union. In keeping with this change of focus, the name "European Economic Community" was done away with, and the "European Union" was born.[25]

- The Treaty of Amsterdam (1997): This treaty, enforced on May 1, 1999, revised the Treaty of the European Union, strengthening the three pillars of the EU. It increased the power of the European Parliament in numerous areas, including economic and immigration decisions. It created a common foreign and security policy. It strengthened police and judicial cooperation. The revisions developed in Amsterdam prepared the EU for their upcoming enlargement.[26]

- The Treaty of Lisbon (2007): As the EU continued to grow, reform was needed to accommodate this expansion. This treaty did some restructuring and adapted how decisions are made. There was also a new function created in the EU institutional architecture: President of the European Council.[27]

Europe still has its divisions, but it is gradually coming together. The recent Brexit movement, which saw the United Kingdom pulling out of the EU, only slowed down this unification process. Much of the prognostication of the 2019 European divorce date is very pessimistic economically for the United Kingdom.[28] This raises the question of how long the British will be willing to stand alone before there is a vote to return to the European fold.

Europe Prepared

Europe is well positioned as the new Babylon. They have kicked God out and invited Babylon in. They have exported satanic worship and a liberal lifestyle. They have promoted globalism, yet they are very anti-Israel. They fit the description remarkably well.

As we saw in Daniel 7:7–8, the little horn is going to come out of this region. Of the rise of the Antichrist, Paul writes,

> Do you not remember that when I was still with you I told you these things? And now you know what is restraining, that he may be revealed in his own time. For the mystery of lawlessness is already at work; only He who now restrains will do so until He is taken out of the way. And then the lawless one will be revealed, whom the Lord will consume with the breath of His mouth and destroy with the brightness of His coming.
>
> 2 Thessalonians 2:5–8

When the Holy Spirit (the Restrainer) is gone, along with the Church, the Antichrist will be revealed. He will deceive the world until the Second Coming when Christ will kill "with the breath of His mouth" this lawless one.

The Antichrist will exist for a limited time in a circumscribed area for a specific target. We, as believers, will not see him because we will already be gone. When we return with Christ, it will be the end of the evil one. One truth the deceiver cannot destroy is that Jesus Christ will have the ultimate victory.

11

Days of Ezekiel 36–37: What Was and What Is

The Discovery Channel used to air a television show called *Dirty Jobs*. On each episode of this program, the host, Mike Rowe, would focus on the people who for a living carried out the occupations that most everyone else in the civilized world would avoid at all costs. He spent time with sewer inspectors, worm dung farmers, skull cleaners and even an avian vomitologist. If Rowe had aired his show in Israel during the Old Testament era, one of the first episodes would have focused on the prophet.

Wanted: One Prophet

Who would ever want to be a prophet? First of all, God often asked them to do very strange things. In order to prove a point, God might have a prophet lie on one side for a year, and then flip over to the other side. God could tell a prophet to cook his food

175

on human dung, walk around naked for three years or marry a prostitute. Not a very glamorous calling. Second, prophets were hated by their people. Rarely were they listened to. More often than not, they were ridiculed, beaten and killed. To step into the role of prophet took a true call from God.

Today, the opposite is often true; how easy it is to be honored and held in high esteem! Many measure the worth of a prophet in book sales and television ratings instead of the quality of the prophecy. Prophets themselves may play on fame and flash and fear, and their greatest asset can be image. Like using a screwdriver handle to pound in a nail, such men and women misuse Scripture to bolster their lies rather than to discover truth.

These false prophets are able to get away with it because no one holds them accountable. I have seen many of them around the world, particularly in Asia. People practically worship them when they step off the plane. They are driven in the finest cars and stay at the finest hotels. Thousands come to hear what they say. Even when their predictions do not come to pass, they are invited back to the next year's conference. Where are the people who will stand up and say, "No! You are a false prophet!"? If we held today's "prophets" to the Old Testament standard of "if a prophet speaks in the name of the Lord presumptuously, and the thing does not come to pass, that prophet shall die," then a lot more false preachers would be dodging rocks (see Deuteronomy 18:20; 28:20–22).

Remember, God wants us to know His plans: "For I am God, and there is no other; I am God, and there is none like Me, declaring the end from the beginning, and from ancient times things that are not yet done, saying, 'My counsel shall stand, and I will do all My pleasure'" (Isaiah 46:9–10). You do not need a modern foretelling prophet to tell you what is going to happen. You just need a Bible! What I am writing in this book is not some new, special revelation; it is not some great discovery that I have uncovered. It is simply what God has told us clearly in His Word.

My passion for biblical prophecy is so great because God's desire for us to know His plans is so great. Nearly one-third of all Scripture is prophetic, starting in the Old Testament and carrying on through the New. Believers must study prophecy, and churches must teach prophecy. Sadly, there is too little going on of either. Too many people write off prophecy as being Old Covenant or irrelevant, but to ignore prophecy is to ignore much of what Jesus taught: "God, who at various times and in various ways spoke in time past to the fathers by the prophets, has in these last days spoken to us by His Son, whom He has appointed heir of all things, through whom also He made the worlds" (Hebrews 1:1–2). Others ignore prophecy out of fear. But the only ones who should be afraid of the "last hour" are unbelievers.

Through God's prophetic Scripture, we understand that God has spoken. His Word shows us how God is at work and helps us comprehend that we live in a world of decay. There are certain smells in this world that are instantly recognizable—and instantly revolting. One of those smells is death and decay. Sniffing around this world, we have no difficulty recognizing that it is deteriorating and heading for a collapse.

The Coming of the Collapses

The first collapse in store for the world is financial. For the last one hundred years, an elite group has controlled the banks. These are the same people who control the media. Certain members of this elite group believe that they are the enlightened ones, knowing best what is right and wrong. Those of us who are unenlightened, the "sheeple," are seen as too dumb to make our own decisions. Thus, the elite feed us, take care of us and tell us what to do.

After decades of carrying out their own agenda, they have the world's economies in place. Money without value or substance floods the global market. A nation's currency used to be backed by something tangible, like gold. That standard gone, economies now float on worthless currencies. This is certainly true of the U.S. economy; before long, the U.S. dollar will deflate, possibly sixty to seventy percent, taking down countless other currencies with it.

In June 2015, the *Telegraph* published an article with headlines that read, "The World Is Defenceless against the Next Financial Crisis, Warns BIS" [Bank of International Settlements—the central bank of the central banks]: Monetary policymakers have run out of room to fight the next crisis with interest rates unable to go lower."[1]

These elites have dug a hole that the world economy will not be able to escape. When the next recession or depression comes, currency will be worth nothing. People will not be able to buy food; rioting around the world will be commonplace. Because of widespread governmental instabilities, a global police force will be needed to regain control.

How will the world's economies restabilize? A global currency will come to the rescue. When everyone has the same currency, then no longer is there a need for economic warfare. Everyone will be working together to serve the financial good of all mankind. The euro, created in 1995 and fully instituted in 1999, could very well be the global currency that the world's financial markets will eventually rally around.

Some may feel that the true danger of a global financial system is the loss of the individual. Welcome to the world of digital! Everyone will be issued a personal identification chip. You will be tied into the vast central computer database, so you can always access your own personal wealth. You can monitor what you have, and the global government will be able to monitor you. The day will soon come when you will not be able to transact any business or have access to any services without that identification chip. Revelation 13:16–17 warns, "He causes all, both small and great, rich and poor, free and slave, to receive a mark on their right hand or on their foreheads, and that no one may buy or sell except one who has the mark or the name of the beast, or the number of his name." At what other time in history would receiving this mark seem so logical and so practical?

The second collapse that this world will experience is physical. In its July 2015 issue, the *New Yorker* published a cover photo depicting the west coast of the United States being torn from the map. Inside, Kathryn Schulz wrote a doomsday article entitled "The Really Big One," which predicted that any day now California could see a 9.2 earthquake. While a temblor that size could reduce many cities to rubble, the quake itself is not the greatest danger. A seismic event of that size could trigger a 700-mile-long, 100-foot-tall tsunami that would completely destroy the Northwest, including Seattle and Tacoma. The takeaway from her article is that it is not a matter of if it will happen, but when.[2]

There is ever-increasing activity on California's San Andreas fault. Even in the heart of America, the New Madrid fault, located in Missouri, is seeing growing movement. These are just examples of what is happening all over the world—more and more earthquakes of ever-increasing intensity.

Not long ago, I was in the Philippines having dental work done. I was waiting for the procedure to begin when everyone suddenly began to leave the building. I was wondering if it was something that I said or maybe they just have an aversion to God's chosen people, when I was told that it was an earthquake drill. The expectation of a seismic disaster has become part of the culture in many earthquake-prone regions.

When the disciples asked Jesus about the end of the age, He did not answer them with discussions of blood moons, the Shemitah or the latest end times prediction. He said,

> And you will hear of wars and rumors of wars. See that you are not troubled; for all these things must come to pass, but the end is not yet. For nation will rise against nation, and kingdom against kingdom. And there will be famines, pestilences, and earthquakes in various places. All these are the beginning of sorrows.
>
> Matthew 24:6–8

The Lord has made it perfectly clear what we should be watching for, but that is not enough for us. We want flash—we want novelty—we want action. We want harbingers and blood moons.

When Joel says, "The sun shall be turned into darkness, and the moon into blood, before the coming of the great and awesome day of the LORD," he is speaking of the time of the Tribulation (Joel 2:31). I do not know about you, but I do not plan on being here when the moon is turned to blood. You can wait for your blood moons; I plan on being raptured. The enemy wants us to focus on the latest theory and get caught up in the newest end times craze because they take us away from the Bible. He would much rather you read someone else's "truth" than God's Truth.

A third area of collapse is political. Leadership instability exists all across the globe. Governmental powers in many countries are being overturned—some by lawful elections and some by force. It seems that the world is longing for a strong leader who will stand up for the people and focus on interests other than his or her own. Throughout the Middle East—and now in Europe and the United States—the political map is shifting.

One result of this shift is the ever-increasing isolation of Israel. In the year 2016, the United Nations adopted twenty anti-Israel resolutions. That statistic alone should make clear the core anti-Semitic beliefs of the UN.

This world has a stench of rot and decay about it. Rather than fear this deterioration, we should keep our eyes on the sky. Clearly, we are in the days of Ezekiel, and the last hour rapidly approaches.

Ezekiel 36: The Return to the Land

These are the days of Ezekiel. We can see the prophecies of Ezekiel 36–39: those that have already taken place, those that are taking place at this present time and those that are about to take place. The return of the Jews to their home triggered this time of joy and tribulation.

As we saw earlier, Israel was a barren wasteland prior to the Jews returning. The land was dead because it was not in the hands of its rightful owners. The few Arabs who were in the misnamed Palestine had let the area turn to marsh and desert. But then the Jews began to come back; with them came God's blessing on the land.

> Thus says the Lord GOD: "On the day that I cleanse you from all your iniquities, I will also enable you to dwell in the cities, and the ruins shall be rebuilt. The desolate land shall be tilled instead of lying desolate in the sight of all who pass by. So they will say, 'This land that was desolate has become like the garden of Eden; and the wasted, desolate, and ruined cities are now fortified and inhabited.' Then the nations which are left all around you shall know that I, the LORD, have rebuilt the ruined places and planted what was desolate. I, the LORD, have spoken it, and I will do it." Thus says the Lord GOD: "I will also let the house of Israel inquire of Me to do this for them: I

will increase their men like a flock. Like a flock offered as holy sacrifices, like the flock at Jerusalem on its feast days, so shall the ruined cities be filled with flocks of men. Then they shall know that I am the LORD."

Ezekiel 36:33–38

The return of the Jews to Israel was not the result of the World Zionist Organization, the Balfour Amendment, the termination of the British Mandate or President Truman's recognition of the Israeli state. It was the hand of the Lord. God promised it, and He fulfilled His promise—pure and simple. When God brought the Jews back, He did not just leave them to suffer in malarial swamps or bake in the deserts. His promise was that "this land that was desolate has become like the garden of Eden."

Not long ago, I led an agricultural tour for a very wealthy Indonesian family. They came in order to learn what made Israel thrive the way it does. In Israel, we have tomato plants that yield ten times more than regular tomato plants. The UN, in a rare moment of non-negativity, recognized that there are more species of fruits and vegetables in Israel than in any other country.

Israel is only the size of New Jersey, but it contains five different climate zones. These qualities did not come into existence when Israel declared independence in 1948; they had always been there. But before Israel's statehood, there was no manifestation of it, no careful utilization of this wonderful gift. That is because the rightful owners were not there. Now, even the desert is blooming in Israel.

Again, this is not man's doing; it is all God's handiwork. He does it to show who He is: "Then they shall know that I am the LORD" (Ezekiel 36:38). The return of the Jews to the land occurred without any official international assistance. Not even America helped in this divine repatriation. God said that He would do it so all would know that *He* brought it to pass.

Even the elimination of regional existential threats was without official international assistance. Let me give you two examples. In 1981, the French were about to sell the Iraqis enough plutonium for a bomb. Why they thought this was a good idea, I will never know. The Iraqis had a nuclear reactor that was about to be "hot," i.e., able to refine nuclear materials. While the world stalled, Israel did not wait. We sent a squadron of F-16s in a mission that became known as Operation Opera, and the nuclear reactor ceased to exist.[3]

A quick aside about those F-16s. They had been recently purchased from the United States. Originally, they were supposed to go to the Shah's government in Iran. Then, the Shah fell and Khomeini rose. The U.S. was certainly not going to send them to the new Iranian government, so they were left with a bunch of unwanted F-16s. Israel stepped in and said, "So sorry you are stuck with all those planes. What if we take them off your hands?" We negotiated and got the planes for half price.[4] How is that for a good Jewish deal?

Imagine if Saddam Hussein had nuclear weapons when the U.S. liberated Kuwait in 1991. Imagine if ISIS had them now. Rather than thanking Israel, however, the world—including the United States—raged against us.[5] Sanctions were imposed; for many months, America refused to sell spare parts for the F-16s. Only years later was Israel thanked for taking that risk.[6]

The second incident took place in 2007. Israel had just launched our new Amos satellite, named after the Old Testament prophet. On this satellite was a very sophisticated camera with a high-powered lens. As we were scanning the region, we discovered a building in the Syrian Desert. Many trucks were seen moving from the seaport to that location—a lot of activity for a building in the middle of nowhere. When we asked what it was, we were told that it was an agricultural farm.

So, we decided to send in a few of our own "farmers." They arrived by helicopter at night. Our "farmers" tested the soil around the building, and found uranium—not a typical agricultural fertilizer, even in the Middle East. Before doing anything, we wanted more confirmation. When the head of the Syrian nuclear program visited Europe, we visited his hotel room. It is amazing all the data that can be pulled off a laptop computer and onto a thumb drive. The information confirmed our suspicions. We asked the United States for help and were told no. So, we acted on our own and destroyed the nuclear reactor they were building.[7]

Again, can you imagine Bashar al-Assad's Syria with a nuclear reactor? Can you envision what the Middle East might look like today if Syria had acquired a nuclear weapon? God promised that He would bring His people back to the land; He is the One who accomplished it to the glory of His name.

Ezekiel 37: The Restoration of the People

One day, the prophet Ezekiel found himself transported by the Holy Spirit into a valley. As he looked around, he discovered that it was full of bones. God asked him, "Can these bones live?" Sensing a trick question, Ezekiel wisely said, "O Lord God, you know." God then told Ezekiel to prophesy skin, breath and life upon this field of bones. Ezekiel did and a rattling began. The bones began piecing themselves together. The hip bone became connected to the thigh bone. The thigh bone became connected to the knee bone. After the giant jigsaw puzzle was completed, sinews and muscles and flesh formed until the valley was filled with a multitude of lifeless bodies.

God said, "Prophesy to the breath, prophesy, son of man, and say to the breath, 'Thus says the Lord God: "Come from the four winds, O breath, and breathe on these slain, that they may live"'" (Ezekiel 37:9). Ezekiel did so, and life entered the lifeless bodies. They stood and were "an exceedingly great army." Then God made a wonderful promise:

> Then He said to me, "Son of man, these bones are the whole house of Israel. They indeed say, 'Our bones are dry, our hope is lost, and we ourselves are cut off!' Therefore prophesy and say to them, 'Thus says the Lord GOD: "Behold, O My people, I will open your graves and cause you to come up from your graves, and bring you into the land of Israel. Then you shall know that I am the LORD, when I have opened your graves, O My people, and brought you up from your graves. I will put My Spirit in you, and you shall live, and I will place you in your own land. Then you shall know that I, the LORD, have spoken it and performed it," says the LORD.'"
>
> Ezekiel 37:11–14

"These bones are the whole house of Israel," the Lord said. These restored bones are God's chosen people. When the Allied forces were liberating the death camps at the end of World War II, what did they find? People who were just skin and bones. Life was barely in them. "Our bones are dry, our hope is lost," they said. When you looked in the eyes of the survivors, there was no hope left. They had been cut off with no future.

But there was hope and a future because God never forgets His promises. The Lord said that He would open their graves; He would bring them back to their land. He would put His Spirit in them and give them life. Why? So they will know that He is the Lord.

Our God is a God whose yea is always yea, and whose nay is always nay. God will keep His promise, even if it occurs by the most circuitous route. Even if this means, for instance, that a boat crammed full of Holocaust survivors is turned away from the Promised Land by the British and forced into a refugee camp

185

in Cyprus before they are finally emigrated. In 1984, Ethiopian Jews were starving in Sudan. An emergency airlift, dubbed Operation Moses, was begun. In total, eight thousand men, women and children were rescued to Israel.[8] Seven years later, Operation Solomon was launched, which brought another 14,500 Ethiopian Jews to the Promised Land in less than 36 hours.[9]

The Lord said, "I will bring you back." He continues to do so.

I am the product of this return. I am a Jew of the tribe of Judah. Once, when I was on the island of Cebu in the Philippines, a group of young girls seemed to keep checking me out. I was flattered until I learned that they just wanted to see what a real Jew looked like. Then, when they heard I was of the tribe of Judah, they stopped listening to my talk and began checking me out again. Not just a Jew, but a Judah Jew! Against all odds, God has maintained His people and brought them back to the land.

Ezekiel 37 has been fulfilled. From the preparation of the land to the establishment of the state, from the rescue of the remnant from the ovens of the Holocaust to the return of those from the Diaspora over the last sixty to seventy years, we have seen more prophecy fulfilled in this generation than at any period since the time of Jesus. Israel exists, and it is safe, secure and prosperous. In my town, I can send my son out to play without fear of kidnapping. I cannot do that in America. Yes, we are still in danger of extermination by those nations surrounding us, but we are strong. And now, when someone attacks, we are in a position to do something about it.

12

Days of Ezekiel 38–39: What Is and What Will Be

I can tell you with certainty that the sun will come up tomorrow. I can tell you with certainty that if I drop a brick on my bare foot, two things will happen: The brick will fall, and I will experience pain. I can tell you with certainty that thousands of Palestinians spent time today discussing the best way to destroy Israel. There are numerous subjects on which we can take a one-hundred-percent definitive stand, saying, "This will happen this way."

Relating biblical prophecy to modern times is not one of those subjects. I will not make definitive claims in this book and declare there are no other options. That is because I am not a prophet; I am a student of the Word of God. What I relate in this chapter is what I have discerned as a man who has spent years studying the Bible, praying through the Scriptures and seeking the truth that the Lord wants us to know about who He is and what He has planned for the last hour. God has also given me a unique perspective as a Jew living in Israel with my house on the edge of the Valley of Armageddon.

Some may argue that I am hedging my bets—giving myself an out if something I write turns out to be inaccurate. Absolutely not. If you read a book where the author claims that he is one-hundred-percent right about his end times views, then he is one-hundred-percent wrong in his assessment of himself. With that caveat, let me say that I truly believe we are currently in the days of Ezekiel 38.

Security and Isolation of Israel

There are two places we need to keep our eyes on today—Israel and Damascus. In these locations, we will see the next triggers being pulled. We can see Israel's isolation growing. The horrible Iran Deal has left the nation by itself. The UN is constantly attacking Israel and blaming it for atrocities. Anti-Semitism is rising all around the world. Jews are being attacked in synagogues, in shops, at home, on the streets, while visiting graveyards and at bar mitzvahs. Do you hear about all these acts of violence? Of course not. But if one Palestinian boy is injured or killed, it is headline news.

In July 2014, *Newsweek* published an article by Adam Lebor entitled, "Exodus: Why Europe's Jews Are Fleeing Once Again." In it, Lebor chronicles anti-Jewish riots in many places across the continent. In one incident in 2014, four hundred protesters in Sarcelles, a northern Paris suburb, "attacked a synagogue and Jewish-owned businesses . . . shouting, 'Death to the Jews.'" In Malmo, Sweden, violence against Jews "tripled between 2010 and 2012," including a bombing at the Jewish community center. In another particularly heinous 2012 attack in Toulouse, France, a gunman entered a Jewish school and killed seven, "including a teacher and three children."[1]

It is no wonder that so many Jews are joining the *aliyah* and returning to Israel.

For the events of Ezekiel 38 to take place, the world needs to be either apathetic or hostile toward the nation of Israel. Currently, both aspects of that description most certainly apply.

We also need to keep our eyes on Damascus, Syria. As we will discuss in a few moments, Damascus will be leveled, a likely catalyst for the rest of the events of Ezekiel 38. It is not difficult to imagine that the same thing that happened to the city of Aleppo might happen to Damascus. The war will move to Damascus because a large store of chemical weapons is hidden underground in the city. In the fight for those armaments, the city will be devastated.

The Battle Begins

The Lord tells us that when Israel feels safe and secure, others will come to take what Israel has:

> Thus says the Lord GOD: "On that day it shall come to pass that thoughts will arise in your mind, and you will make an evil plan: You will say, 'I will go up against a land of unwalled villages; I will go to a peaceful people, who dwell safely, all of them dwelling without walls, and having neither bars nor gates'—to take plunder and to take booty, to stretch out your hand against the waste places that are again inhabited, and against a people gathered from the nations, who have acquired livestock and goods, who dwell in the midst of the land."
>
> Ezekiel 38:10–12

The nation of Israel is the "gathered people" who are dwelling securely. But who is coming to attack? Ezekiel lays out the players very clearly.

The first and primary player we must identify is Gog of the land of Magog:

> Now the word of the LORD came to me, saying, "Son of man, set your face against Gog, of the land of Magog, the prince of Rosh, Meshech, and Tubal, and prophesy against him, and say, 'Thus says the Lord GOD: Behold, I am against you, O Gog, the prince of Rosh, Meshech, and Tubal. I will turn you around, put hooks into your jaws, and lead you out, with all your army, horses, and horsemen, all splendidly clothed, a great company with bucklers and shields, all of them handling swords.'"
>
> Ezekiel 38:1–4

In old Arabic, the Great Wall of China was called the wall of Al Magog. Other ancient writers referred to the wall as "*Sud Yagog et Magog*, that is, the mud wall, or rampart of Gog and Magog."[2] Why was the Great Wall of China built? To keep out the forces of Gog and Magog, which came from part of the area that now makes up Russia. In the course of my own Bible research, I have found that many names exist for Russia—Magog, Rosh, Meshech, Tubal—and for its leader—Gog.

Russia misses its days of being a major empire, and Vladimir Putin wants to become the new tsar. The recovery of the country's former global importance, if not of its former economic strength, has been remarkable. Putin has grasped a firm hold on his nation and on the surrounding regions. His theft of Crimea and invasion into Ukraine were met with diplomatic slaps on the wrist because there was no one around to stand up to him. Now he is calling the shots in the Middle East. In December 2016, a cease-fire in Syria was arranged by Russia. In the past, such pacts were formalized in Washington, D.C. This time, the U.S. was not even invited to the negotiations. Currently, Israeli intelligence is picking up more Russian than Arabic in Syria.

"Wait, Amir," you say. "Are you saying that Vladimir Putin is Gog?" No, but he could be. He fits the mold, but to assign the name *Gog* to any person without more evidence would be speculation.

Russia will lead the attack against Israel. What Gog, the leader of Russia, thinks is an expression of his own great power is really just an act of his subservience to the all-powerful God: "Behold, I am against you, O Gog, the prince of Rosh, Meshech, and Tubal. I will turn you around, put hooks into your jaws, and lead you out" (Ezekiel 38:3–4). God will lead this powerful leader around like a captive with a hook through his jaw. Even when it looks like evil might be winning, God is still in control.

Russia's partner in this attack will be Persia—modern-day Iran. The Western world knows very little about Iran, except that it has absolutely no clue how Iran thinks. In other words, when the West understands that they cannot understand Iran, only then will they begin to understand Iran.

The Iran Deal orchestrated by the Barack Obama administration was a perfect example. The U.S. went into the deal actually believing there was a good chance Iran would honor their commitment. Iran had no such intention. While the West assumed that Iran would hold off on nuclear weapons for ten years, Iran was thinking, "How can we get them tomorrow?" In ten years, someone would come up with other reasons why they should not have nuclear arms. In the meantime, they would have a decade-long window wherein the West would essentially be off their backs. As a result of the Iran Deal, they were allowed to keep all their facilities and five thousand centrifuges—what do you think they will be using them for?

But were not monitoring structures put in place? Yes, if you can call them that. If a monitoring team requests to visit a nuclear site, it can take 24 days before that team is allowed on site. What do you think the Iranians are doing during that window of time? Maybe they need the three-and-a-half weeks to tidy the place up? Maybe they want to make sure that all the employee uniforms are cleaned and pressed? Or just maybe they will use that time to hide any evidence of what they are truly doing?

If a monitoring team requests a soil sample from the area surrounding a nuclear facility, who do you think provides it? "Well, Mr. Iranian Nuclear Person, the soil sample you provided has a very high content of nitrites similar to that found in the fertilizers for common potted plants. Are you sure it came from the nuclear site and not from a bag of potting soil?" If a monitoring team makes an appeal against something the Iranians have done, it takes months for it to be adjudicated.

Meanwhile, Iran did not have to wait for sanctions to be lifted from them. That was immediate. And, as a bonus, the United States decided to pass on billions of (do not call them ransom) dollars that the government even admitted would likely be used for terrorism. Then Secretary of State John Kerry tried to ease our minds, though. In response to Iran's regular policy of chanting "Death to America," he responded, "I think they have a policy of opposition to us and a great enmity, but I have no specific knowledge of a plan by Iran to actually destroy us."[3]

I guess it depends on what one's definition of "death" is.

Why is Iran so determined to acquire a nuclear weapon? They want the strength and leverage of being part of the nuclear club. Surprisingly, the one who should fear this course the most is not the United States and Israel, but Saudi Arabia. Iran hates the West, and they despise Israel—but they loathe the Saudis ten times more. The reason for this all comes down to the brand of Islam they follow. The Saudis are the guardians of Sunni Islam, and the Iranian Shiites detest them as only a religious fanatic can detest someone they believe is a heretic. That does not mean that Israel is in the clear; it just means that the first bomb may not drop on us.

People ask me when Israel is going to attack the Iranian nuclear facilities. I do not know; I am not the prime minister. What I do know is that when Israel attacks, the world may not even know it. There are other ways to destroy a nuclear facility than bombing it. Why send an F-16 when you can send a virus?

Back in 2009, when Iran's nuclear program was beginning to take off, a joint Israeli-U.S. operation delivered a thumb drive to an employee in the nation's nuclear department. This employee, who was really an Iranian double agent, inserted that drive into his computer, which then loaded a virus called Stuxnet into the system. This virus told the centrifuges to work five times faster, while telling the main control that everything was fine. It was not long before the centrifuges burned out.[4]

In 2012, using the cover of a Microsoft software upgrade, Israel and the United States inserted the Flame virus into the computer system of the Iranian nuclear facilities. This virus allowed us to see what was on the screens of their computers.[5] As we looked around, whenever we found very important information, we would make good use of the "delete" button. But we did not stop there. Sometimes, rather than deleting that important information, we would change it up a bit. Turn some good information into bad information. When Iran finally discovered the hack, they had no idea what information was accurate and what was altered. Iran cannot be allowed to have a nuclear weapon, and Israel will do whatever is necessary to make sure it does not happen.

Iran (Persia) will join Russia in an attack against Israel: "Persia, Ethiopia, and Libya are with them, all of them with shield and helmet; Gomer and all its troops; the house of Togarmah from the far north and all its troops—many people are with you" (Ezekiel 38:5–6). We have already seen Iran and Russia teaming up in Syria. When the United States rained 59 cruise missiles down onto a Syrian airfield after a horrible chemical weapon attack, Russia and Iran stood united with Syria in their condemnation of America. If, in the future, something does happen against Damascus, these two allies will go in together all the way.

Why does Russia care about Israel to begin with? It all comes down to gas. They really do not care about the Palestinian/Israeli conflict or religious ideologies. Vladimir Putin has never been particularly known for his altruism or his faith. Russia wants to be the number one gas supplier in the world.

Israel had managed to stay off Russia's radar for many decades, but something changed four or five years ago. Israel discovered trillions of cubic feet of natural gas just off our Mediterranean coast. That vaulted us from being primarily an energy importer to one of the world's chief energy concerns. Suddenly, Putin was making a state visit to Israel. He came asking Prime Minister Netanyahu for a partnership in this enormous gas reserve. Netanyahu told him, "*Dasvidaniya.*" Putin is not a man who enjoys hearing *no*, and when he has an excuse, he will be back to take what we refused to give to him.

Another nation that Ezekiel mentions joining the attack is Cush, also known as Ethiopia. Ethiopia now is not the same as Ethiopia then. In the time of Ezekiel, Cush was the region now known as Sudan. It is not surprising to see Sudan as part of this alliance, considering the relationships that exist today. The same ideological and relational affinities hold true for Put (Libya).

Iran and Sudan are very close. Iran gives money to Sudan, and Sudan lets Iran orchestrate terrorism through their nation. Five times in the last four years, Israel has struck Sudan. Each time it was for allowing Iran to smuggle weapons through their country and on to Sinai and Gaza. Iran built a factory in Khartoum, the capital city, in order to manufacture rockets so that they do not have to ship their own to the Palestinians.

Israel destroyed that plant as well. When Israel needs to strike, we do not sit around and talk about it. When you need to shoot, you shoot. Talking comes later.

Not long ago, Israeli intelligence tapped some vital Sudanese phones. They heard Iranian and North Korean scientists talking; no Sudanese were even on the line. Israel is at the top of Sudan's bad list, and they will jump at the chance to join the alliance.

One more nation that will join against Israel is Turkey. In Ezekiel, *Gomer* and *Togarmah* refer to Turkey. While Israel used to have a great ally in this region, the situation has altered greatly with the election of Recep Tayyip Erdogan as president in 2014. He brought a much more radical Islamic mindset to the government. The number of mosques built in the last two years in Turkey is more than the last seventy years combined. While he is playing nicely right now because Israel is looking to build a gas pipeline across Turkey to Europe, he will jump at the chance to join any alliance that brings an end to the Zionist/Israeli entity.

There are a few other nations that are mentioned in Ezekiel 38:

> Sheba, Dedan, the merchants of Tarshish, and all their young lions will say to you, "Have you come to take plunder? Have you gathered your army to take booty, to carry away silver and gold, to take away livestock and goods, to take great plunder?"
>
> Ezekiel 38:13

These nations are looking on, criticizing the attack on Israel, but they will not do anything about it.

Sheba and *Dedan* refer to Saudi Arabia. While most nations are distancing themselves from Israel, the Saudis are actually becoming friendlier. This friendship is not official, but is built on an understanding of a mutual threat in a nuclear Iran. The "merchants of Tarshish" speaks of Europe. Tarshish, familiar to many as the destination that Jonah sought to flee to, is in Spain. As the current general attitude of the UN demonstrates, Europe is all talk and no action.

Many people want to know where the United States is in the Bible. How does this great power fit into the days of Ezekiel? I believe we see America in this passage, identified in some translations as the "leaders of Tarshish." The word translated "leaders" is actually Hebrew for "young lions."

Europe is the established guard, while the Americans are the young lions that were birthed out of the loins of the old world. Unfortunately, the U.S. has joined with its ancestors in irrelevance in the Middle East. After orchestrating a United Nations vote against Israel in 2016 condemning Jewish settlements, Secretary of State John Kerry made this remarkable statement: "If the choice is one state, Israel can be Jewish or democratic. It cannot be both."[6] America has essentially separated from Israel. They will huff and puff, but will not act.

With the new administration, we in Israel are hopeful for an improved relationship between the U.S. and Israel. Donald Trump has said some very encouraging words. However, history and the temporary nature of U.S. presidencies cause us to maintain a wait-and-see attitude, particularly as we look long-term. Even with Donald Trump in the White House, if we are ever attacked, we expect to be fighting our military battles alone.

Russia, Iran, Turkey and Sudan are ready to attack Israel. They are just waiting for the match that will light the fire. I am not a prophet; I am just looking at the Scriptures. As I mentioned earlier, I believe that the destruction of Damascus will be that match. Syria is the one thing that has brought all of these nations together. The chemical weapons stash buried in Damascus will be the hand that strikes the match.

Up until recently, it would have been hard to imagine these countries allying together. The three primary actors, Russia, Iran and Turkey, could not stand each other. Suddenly, they are all friends. Russia and Turkey just signed a pact to let oil flow from Russia to Europe through Turkey. This oil used to go through Ukraine, but now the Russians feel that they cannot trust that route. So, Turkey is sitting in the catbird seat, with Israel and Russia both wanting to send their gas through them. This is where the clash between Israel and Russia will originate. Russia wants exclusivity, particularly in those European markets that Israel is looking to tap. Russia needs the gas money; it is the only thing propping up their failing economy. If Israel is a threat to that, then Israel will have to go. No one ever anticipated this scenario; Ezekiel 38, however, has laid out these future events.

When the battle begins, it will usher in a world war. Three continents will be represented by the aggressors. While it will not be as vast in scope, population-wise, as other world wars, it will be immense in area. It is interesting to note that much of World War II was about destroying the Jews in the Holocaust. World War III will be about destroying Jews in their homeland. Look at how hard Satan is trying to kill the Jews!

I have mentioned several times that I believe that Damascus will be the spark that touches off the explosion of this great battle against Israel. The prophet Isaiah warns us of the utter destruction of this city prior to the events of the last hour: "The burden against Damascus. 'Behold, Damascus will cease from being a city, and it will be a ruinous heap'" (Isaiah 17:1). An aerial view of Damascus today reveals a city gradually deteriorating through ongoing warfare. But this is a vast city; its destruction is not yet complete. Isaiah says that it will become "a heap of ruins." All we need to do is look at Aleppo to see the kind of devastation Isaiah refers to. When the demolition of Damascus matches that of Aleppo, all hell will break loose.

13

WHAT IS NEXT?

In this final chapter, we will answer the two questions that tend to stand out in most people's minds as they approach the last hour: "What is next?" and "So what?" In other words, what should I be watching for, and what does it mean to me? We have dealt with both of these questions in different ways throughout this book. Here, I will seek to give you an overview of the order of coming events. My prayer is that you will remember the theme with which we started this book: If you are right with the Lord, you do not have to be afraid. Rather than causing consternation, these words should give you a deep sense of peace. God is in control, and if Jesus is your Lord and Savior, then you are safely in His hands.

So Much Confusion

If you are looking for dates for what is coming next, you are going to be sorely disappointed. What we *can* know is the order of events. All we need to do is to look at the Bible and treat it as the literal Word of God. So many Christians get confused about what is next because they take random passages of Scripture and mix them around until, as my friends in the Philippines say, they become chicken adobo (and smell like durian). The Bible was written as a whole. When we interpret it as a whole, rather than as random pieces of information, then the timeline begins to come into shape.

This is part of the reason why the disciples were so clueless when it came to the two comings of the Messiah. They thought these events would occur at the same time: Jesus would come riding into Jerusalem as both Messiah and King. But when Jesus spoke of His comings, it was with the understanding that there would be two fulfillments: one that He carried out as Messiah in His time on earth, and one when He returns as the King of kings during the time of Jacob's trouble (the Tribulation).

But it was not Jesus alone who spoke of the two comings of Christ. The Old Testament makes it clear that the first coming of the Messiah would involve His suffering, death and resurrection. His return would rescue His people, Israel, after a harsh period of trouble and tribulation.

Interestingly, the Talmud says that the first time the Messiah comes, He will be on a donkey, yet the people will not be ready for Him. The second time He comes, He will be on a horse, and then the people will be ready for Him. When Jesus rode into Jerusalem on the donkey, He was not celebrating. There was no elation. He understood that His children, who had been anxiously expecting a Messiah, had missed the Messiah in their midst. He had come "to His own, and His own did not receive Him" (John 1:11). When He returns on horseback, all His people will see Him for who He is.

Now I saw heaven opened, and behold, a white horse. And He who sat on him was called Faithful and True, and in righteousness

He judges and makes war. His eyes were like a flame of fire, and on His head were many crowns. He had a name written that no one knew except Himself. He was clothed with a robe dipped in blood, and His name is called The Word of God. And the armies in heaven, clothed in fine linen, white and clean, followed Him on white horses. Now out of His mouth goes a sharp sword, that with it He should strike the nations. And He Himself will rule them with a rod of iron. He Himself treads the winepress of the fierceness and wrath of Almighty God. And He has on His robe and on His thigh a name written:

KING OF KINGS AND LORD OF LORDS.

Revelation 19:11–16

Can we blame the disciples for misunderstanding the comings of the Messiah? No, they did not have all the information. We have all the information, so we are without excuse. We need to make sure that we use the information properly, as a whole, because if major doctrines of the Bible such as the first and second comings of Christ could be misunderstood by those who were closest to Him, we certainly can fall into the pit of misinterpretation and misunderstanding. As I lay this out, please remember that I am no prophet; I just study the Bible.

The Timeline

The prophecies of Ezekiel 36 and most of Ezekiel 37 have come to pass. In Ezekiel 36, God promised that He would restore the land of Israel. He has done so. From the late nineteenth century, when the Jews began resettling, till now, the land has transformed from a barren, swampy wasteland to a lush, thriving, wealthy country. Through the blessings of God and the hard work of the people, Israel has once again become a strong, self-sustaining, independent nation.

Not only did God promise to restore the land, but He gave His word that He would bring back His people. In Ezekiel 37, God gives the prophet a vision of a valley of dry bones being reborn and rejuvenated. This very thing has happened as Jews who were scattered around the world are returning to their Promised Land. The Lord even used the horror of the Holocaust to move the international community finally to acquiesce to a Jewish homeland in a perfect illustration of the ways He brings beauty from ashes.

Immediately, Satan attacked. Remember, before the devil is bound and thrown into the bottomless pit, all Israel will be saved (see Romans 11:26). The last thing he wants is for God's people to have a united nation with a united identity. So, as soon as independence was declared in 1948, all the first-tier countries—those with mutual borders to Israel—threw the full measure of their military might against the fledgling country. Unsurprisingly, this assault fits right into biblical prophecy. The psalmist Asaph writes,

> Do not keep silent, O God! Do not hold Your peace, and do not be still, O God! For behold, Your enemies make a tumult; and those who hate You have lifted up their head. They have taken crafty counsel against Your people, and consulted together against Your sheltered ones. They have said, "Come, and let us cut them off from being a nation, that the name of Israel may be remembered no more." For they have consulted together with one consent; they form a confederacy against You: the tents of Edom and the Ishmaelites; Moab and the Hagrites; Gebal, Ammon, and Amalek; Philistia with the inhabitants of Tyre; Assyria also has joined with them; they have helped the children of Lot.
>
> Psalm 83:1–8

The Lord answered the prayer of Asaph, and He answered the prayers of the Israelis in 1948. There is no way the army of this new nation could have defeated this coalition of states. But God could, and God did. This battle for independence was not won because of what took place on the battlefield, but in spite of it.

Since that time, these first-tier nations have been defeated over and over whenever they went up against Israel: the Suez Crisis (1956), the Six-Day War (1967), the War of Attrition (1967–70), the Yom Kippur War (1973) and the Lebanon Wars (1982; 2006). Along with these wars, there has been consistent battling with the Palestinians in the Intifadas (1987–93; 2000–05) and the conflicts in Gaza (2008–09; 2012; 2014). There have not been many years of peace for the nation of Israel, but through it all, God has cared for His people.

Not only has Israel survived these attacks, some of its first-tier enemies have become friends. A new relationship has begun with both Jordan and Egypt, which, again, fits right into Bible prophecy. Revelation 12 implies that the remnant of the Jews will flee to Jordan during the time of the Tribulation. Isaiah speaks of a highway between Israel and Egypt. The Lord will bring Egypt to repentance, and this highway will bring worshipers of the one true God from the south and the north into Jerusalem.

> In that day there will be a highway from Egypt to Assyria, and the Assyrian will come into Egypt and the Egyptian into Assyria, and the Egyptians will serve with the Assyrians. In that day Israel will be one of three with Egypt and Assyria—a blessing in the midst of the land, whom the LORD of hosts shall bless, saying, "Blessed is Egypt My people, and Assyria the work of My hands, and Israel My inheritance."
>
> Isaiah 19:23–25

Now that these first-tier nations have either been defeated or become friends, it is time for the second-tier nations to attack.

These are the nations beyond Israel's borders—and this will be the next big event on the timeline. As we have seen, the fuse is lit in Damascus: "The burden against Damascus. 'Behold, Damascus will cease from being a city, and it will be a ruinous heap'" (Isaiah 17:1). This devastation has not happened yet, but it is coming. That Syria has become the center of violence and world attention is no coincidence.

The fires of Damascus will be a light that draws the nations in. Some of the countries who were involved in the Syrian conflict will look a little farther south and set their sights on Israel. We Israelis, who for the first thirty years of our existence did not know if we were going to survive until the next week, are now more secure and comfortable than we have ever been. We have gas, oil and all sorts of weapons. (If I told you about them, I would probably have to kill you.) At this coming moment, God will whistle for these nations, particularly Russia, to come.

> Thus says the Lord GOD: "On that day it shall come to pass that thoughts will arise in your mind, and you will make an evil plan: You will say, 'I will go up against a land of unwalled villages; I will go to a peaceful people, who dwell safely, all of them dwelling without walls, and having neither bars nor gates'—to take plunder and to take booty, to stretch out your hand against the waste places that are again inhabited, and against a people gathered from the nations, who have acquired livestock and goods, who dwell in the midst of the land."
>
> Ezekiel 38:10–12

As Ezekiel predicts, these nations will come to steal and plunder. Up until five years ago, Israel did not have much to steal other than falafel and hummus. Now, we have oil and gas, and a whole lot of it. Russia will come with Turkey, Iran and Sudan. Once again, God will fight for Israel, and the Russian alliance will be destroyed in Israel—but not before a horrific battle and a lot of carnage. At some point during this battle, conventional weapons will likely be abandoned and nuclear weapons employed. The fact that they will bury every last bone for seven months and burn the weapons for seven years seems to indicate that radiation must be dealt with:

> Then those who dwell in the cities of Israel will go out and set on fire and burn the weapons, both the shields and bucklers, the bows and arrows, the javelins and spears; and they will make fires with them for seven years. . . . For seven months the house of Israel will be burying them, in order to cleanse the land.
>
> Ezekiel 39:9, 12

Soon after this battle, the Antichrist will arise out of Europe promising peace. The world will be aching for this message after what has taken place in Israel. The Antichrist will bring the nations of the world together. Then, halfway through the seven years of the Tribulation, he will show his true colors. This is the beginning of Jacob's Troubles, when God's wrath begins to be poured out on the world. The Tribulation will culminate in the gathering of armies in Armageddon and a march to the final war that centers on Jerusalem and the Antichrist. The Lord will take the victory and usher in the Millennium.

Peace, Not as the World Gives

If any of this sounds frightening to you, it should not, unless you plan on still being around for these events. As for me, I plan on being long gone when God's wrath hits mankind. If you have Jesus Christ as your Savior and Lord, then you will have been raptured before any of this takes place. Right now, the Holy Spirit is holding back the rise of the Antichrist: "And now you know what is restraining, that he may be revealed in his own time. For the mystery of lawlessness is already at work; only He who now restrains will do so until He is taken out of the way" (2 Thessalonians 2:6–7). When the Holy Spirit—the Restrainer—pulls out, the Church pulls out with Him because there cannot be a Church without the Holy Spirit. Not only is God's plan biblical, it is logical. Why do we get so confused over the Scriptures? God was not confused when He wrote them.

While judgment is taking place on earth, we will be celebrating the marriage ceremony of Christ to the Church, His Bride. At the end of the Tribulation, when Jesus carries out His Second Coming, we will return with Him. This event ushers in the one-thousand-year reign of Christ, ending in a final military defeat for Satan. The Lord's final judgment against all the spirits and people who rejected Him will be carried out, followed by the creation of a new heaven and a new earth.

Hallelujah, we are not destined for God's wrath. We are taken when it is about to begin; we will return when it is about to come to an end.

Time to Get Ready

When I married my beautiful wife, she did not wake up the morning of our wedding, rummage through the closet for something to wear, give her hair a quick run-through with her fingers and head off for the ceremony. There were weeks—months even—spent in preparation for the service. Then, on the day of our wedding, she put hours into preparing herself to be presented to her groom. I feel honored and blessed whenever I think of the effort she put in just so she could look her best for me.

The marriage of the Church to our Savior is coming soon. We need to prepare ourselves even now.

And I heard, as it were, the voice of a great multitude, as the sound of many waters and as the sound of mighty thunderings, saying, "Alleluia! For the Lord God Omnipotent reigns! Let us be glad and rejoice and give Him glory, for the marriage of the Lamb has come, and His wife has made herself ready." And to her it was granted to be arrayed in fine linen, clean and bright, for the fine linen is the righteous acts of the saints.

Revelation 19:6–8

This marriage is the culmination of God's great plan of redemption. What started in Genesis ends in Revelation, and from beginning to end, it is all about Jesus. God created humanity, humanity fell, God promised a Savior, the Savior came and died and rose again so humanity could be reconciled to God and spend an eternity with Him, the Savior left to prepare a place for His Bride, He will call His Bride to Himself, the Savior will marry His Bride and they will live happily ever after for all eternity. It is a real-life storybook ending.

As we can see by the world around us, it is very possible that our time here on earth is short. Thus, it is time to start getting ready. Paul writes,

And do this, knowing the time, that now it is high time to awake out of sleep; for now our salvation is nearer than when we first believed. The night is far spent, the day is at hand. Therefore let us cast off the works of darkness, and let us put on the armor of light. Let us walk properly, as in the day, not in revelry and drunkenness, not in lewdness and lust, not in strife and envy. But put on the Lord Jesus Christ, and make no provision for the flesh, to fulfill its lusts.

Romans 13:11–14

Now is the time for us to wake up from our spiritual slumber. Too many Christians just skate through life, not taking their salvation seriously. They look at salvation only as a blessing and miss the fact that it is also a responsibility.

Churches, too, are asleep. They have gotten comfortable. Pastors preach messages designed to tickle the ears and fill the offering plates. Few preach Bible prophecy because it is confusing and uncomfortable. And the end times are usually sensationalized or fictionalized on the rare occasions they are discussed. Our churches, along with those who attend them, need to teach and spread the truth; we do not have time to fool around. As Paul wrote, our salvation from these bodies is near. The night is almost over, and our day with God is about to begin.

Are you ready? Do you know Jesus and His suffering and the power of His resurrection? Have you accepted the free gift of His salvation? To possess God's perfect peace and the promise of eternity with Him costs us nothing—but we must willingly give everything. We read in the letter to the Ephesians, "For by grace you have been saved through faith, and that not of yourselves; it is the gift of God, not of works, lest anyone should boast" (Ephesians 2:8–9). No grand, heavenly scale exists that balances your good works against your bad deeds. If you are trying to prove yourself to God or earn your salvation, stop. It will not work. You can never do enough to pay for your sins. The wonderful thing is that you do not have to; the price has already been paid. Peter writes, "For Christ also suffered once for sins, the just for the unjust, that He might bring us to God, being put to death in the flesh but made alive by the Spirit" (1 Peter 3:18).

Salvation is as near to you as an acceptance of Jesus as your Savior and your Lord. Determine to trust Him alone to forgive your sins and reconcile you to God. Make Him your Lord—a word that means "Master." Your commitment, then, is to make Jesus the center of your life and follow Him for the rest of your days. When you do that, He does not promise that life will be ducks and bunnies for the rest of your time on earth. In fact, He promises the opposite. Hard times will come. But through them all, He will be there, giving you peace and joy and surrounding you with never-ending love. When your life is over—or when the Church's time on this earth has come to an end—you will be with your God for eternity.

To those who have made this salvation commitment, I ask the same question: Are you ready? Are you following the lead of the Holy Spirit each day? In Galatians, we read, "If we live in the Spirit, let us also walk in the Spirit" (Galatians 5:25). The Holy Spirit has given us new life, and we need to strive to follow His lead day by day. This means seeking His will every day, committing each day to Him and being watchful for opportunities He gives us to share the truth of Christ and partner with Him. It means living the way God has called us to live—not in the old ways of sin and complacency, but in the new ways of the Spirit (see Galatians 5:16–26).

Are you reading your Bible? God has given us His Word for a reason. If your Bible only gets opened on Sundays at church, then you are missing one of the greatest gifts that He has given to you. You cannot be prepared to share the truth of Scripture if you do not know Scripture yourself. And be assured, time spent in God's Word nullifies much of the fear and doubt that many Christians struggle with. Fear is not the birthright of His children.

Are you praying daily? Under the Old Covenant, the people had to go through priests to communicate with God. But now all believers are priests; we have direct access to the Creator God: "Let us therefore come boldly to the throne of grace, that we may obtain mercy and find grace to help in time of need" (Hebrews 4:16). The idea of drawing near to the throne of God would have blown away an Old Testament Israelite. For us, though, it can become mundane. We do not know what it is like to be without prayer. We must not lose sight of the wonder of being able to talk directly to our God, and having Him actually care about what we say. Are you taking advantage of your opportunity to speak to God? Through prayer, you will find your power to serve the Lord. Through prayer, you will find your peace in the midst of life's difficulties.

Are you going about your Father's business? We are here on this earth on a mission. That mission is not to accumulate wealth or see the world or live comfortably or be happy. We are here to serve God. There is nothing wrong if, while serving the Lord, He blesses you with wealth or happiness. But those things are just the gravy; they are not the meal. Paul writes, "For we are His workmanship, created in Christ Jesus for good works, which God prepared beforehand that we should walk in them" (Ephesians 2:10). God has a checklist of "good works" prepared for each of us to accomplish in this lifetime, including lives He wants us to touch, sacrifices He wants us to make, truths He wants us to speak, blessings He wants us to bestow. We each have a personal and unique mission from God; that is why we are here. In business, if a person focuses only on the perks and not on the job, he will get fired. Let us focus on the job God has given us, especially as time gets shorter.

Do you trust God in the good times and the bad? As the time of Christ's return draws near, it is going to get worse for Christians before it gets better. No matter what happens in our lives, whether our faith brings persecution or we simply suffer pain from living in a fallen world, we must keep our eyes on God. He will walk us through the difficulties and grow us through the hard times.

> And not only that, but we also glory in tribulations, knowing that tribulation produces perseverance; and perseverance, character; and character, hope. Now hope does not disappoint,

because the love of God has been poured out in our hearts by the Holy Spirit who was given to us.

Romans 5:3–5

We are all going to suffer at times in this life; let us choose to grow through our suffering. When we see the world going crazy around us, we need to remember that God has a plan for us that involves blessing and not wrath.

Are you truly abiding in God by serving Him? As I mentioned earlier, we need to be in the Word of God. But there is also a time to work. After the Israelites miraculously defeated Jericho, they moved on to the city of Ai. When they attacked, the Israelites were summarily trounced. The army fled back to camp, and the nation went into a state of national panic. Joshua himself was stunned. He went before the Ark of the Covenant and prayed, seeking the Lord's wisdom as to what had just happened. God's reply is as wonderful as it is surprising: "So the LORD said to Joshua: 'Get up! Why do you lie thus on your face? Israel has sinned'" (Joshua 7:10–11). Where else does God tell someone, "Hey, quit your praying and do something!"? A man named Achan had stolen some of the beautiful things from Jericho that were supposed to have been burned as an offering to God. There was sin in the camp, and Joshua was not going to solve the issue by staying down on his knees. Ecclesiastes 3 tells us that there is a time for everything. There is a time to read our Bibles and a time to pray. And there is also a time to take what we have learned in the Word and on our knees out into the world, and put it to good use. Christians, we must not get so insular that our light gets hidden under a basket and we become irrelevant to the world.

Finally, are you supporting Israel? The promise that God gave to Abraham to bless those who bless him and curse those who curse him is an eternal promise. This promise did not end with the exile of Israel; it did not end with the Old Covenant or with the first-century dispersion of the Jews. At minimum, the Church needs to be praying daily for Israel. Christians should also look for ways to take their support a tangible step further, encouraging their governments to support Israel financially or personally choosing to support in a financial way ministries that reach out specifically to the Jewish people. God sees, He knows and He has promised that He will bless.

Shalom

My goal in writing this book is not to cause fear but to bring peace. Fear comes from the unknown. Peace comes from understanding God's plan and seeing that He has things completely under control. I pray that as you finish this book, a *hallelujah* will be on your lips.

We are in the last hour. The countdown clock is nearing zero. While time winds down for the world, the hands on our clock are moving in the other direction. The apostle John writes, "He who has the Son has life; he who does not have the Son of God does not have life. These things I have written to you who believe in the name of the Son of God, that you may know that you have eternal life" (1 John 5:12–13). If Jesus Christ is your Lord and Savior, you have eternal life. *Have* is a present tense verb, meaning you have it right now. Eternal life is not something you are waiting for; it is not something that you will receive when this life is over. Your eternal life is a reality as you are reading these words today. No matter what happens in the days you have left on earth, you have assurance of an eternal life with Christ.

I leave you with the words of Jesus that opened this book:

Peace I leave with you, My peace I give to you; not as the world gives do I give to you. Let not your heart be troubled, neither let it be afraid. You have heard Me say to you, "I am going away and coming back to you." If you loved Me, you would rejoice because I said, "I am going to the Father," for My Father is greater than I. And now I have told you before it comes, that when it does come to pass, you may believe.

John 14:27–29

NOTES

Chapter 1: Looking Back before Looking Forward

1. Ed Hindson, *15 Future Events That Will Shake the World* (Eugene, Ore.: Harvest House, 2014), Kindle edition, introduction.

Chapter 3: Understanding Prophecy: Two-by-Two

1. Andrew Walker, "Why Use Negative Interest Rates?" BBC News, February 15, 2016, http://www.bbc.com/news/business-32284393.

2. Thomas C. Frohlich, Alexander Kent, and Sam Stebbins, "Seven Countries Near Bankruptcy," *USA Today*, August 8, 2015, https://www.usatoday.com/story/money/business/2015/08/05/24-7-wall-st-countries-near-bankruptcy/31164239/.

Chapter 5: Israel: Still God's Chosen People

1. Center for Reformed Theology and Apologetics, "Westminster Shorter Catechism with Proof Texts," CRTA, accessed January 29, 2018, http://www.reformed.org/documents/wsc/index.html?_top=http%3A%2F%2Fwww.reformed.org%2Fdocuments%2FWSC.html.

2. Commission for Religious Relations with the Jews, "'The Gifts and the Calling of God Are Irrevocable' (Rom 11:29): A Reflection on Theological Questions Pertaining to Catholic-Jewish Relations on the Occasion of the 50th Anniversary of 'Nostra Aetate' (NO.4)," Libreria Editrice Vaticana (Vatican Publishing House), December 10, 2015, http://www.vatican.va/roman_curia/pontifical_councils/chrstuni/relations-jews-docs/rc_pc_chrstuni_doc_20151210_ebraismo-nostra-aetate_en.html.

Chapter 6: The Deception of the Nations

1. Ilan Evyatar, "Israel's Economy: Reasons to be Cheerful—and Some for Concern," *Jerusalem Post*, April 27, 2016, http://www.jpost.com/opinion/israels-economy-reasons-to-be-cheerful-and-some-for-concern-452550.

2. "Ancient Jewish History: The Bar-Kokhba Revolt (132–135 CE)," Jewish Virtual Library, accessed February 12, 2018, http://www.jewishvirtuallibrary.org /the-bar-kokhba-revolt-132-135-ce.

3. Mark Twain, *The Innocents Abroad* (Salt Lake City: Project Gutenberg, 2006), Kindle edition, chapter 47.

4. Mitchel Bard, "Pre-State Israel: The Arabs in Palestine," Jewish Virtual Library, accessed February 12, 2018, www.jewishvirtuallibrary.org/the-arabs -in-palestine.

5. Bernard Gwertzman, review of *From Time Immemorial: The Origins of the Arab-Jewish Conflict over Palestine*, by Joan Peters, "Arabs against Jews," *New York Times*, May 12, 1984, www.nytimes.com/1984/05/12/books/books-of-the -times-arabs-against-jews.html.

6. Joan Peters, *From Time Immemorial: The Origins of the Arab-Jewish Conflict over Palestine* (New York: Harper & Row, 1984).

7. Zuheir Mohsen, quoted in James Dorsey, "Wij zijn alleen Palestijn om politieke reden," *Trouw*, March 31, 1977.

8. Bard, "Pre-State Israel: The Arabs in Palestine."

9. Fred J. Khouri, *The Arab-Israeli Dilemma* (Syracuse: Syracuse UP, 1986), 9.

10. Sharif Hussein, *Al-Qibla*, March 23, 1918, quoted in Samuel Katz, *Battleground: Fact and Fantasy in Palestine* (New York: Bantam Books, 1977), 128.

11. "Selected Quotes from Golda Meir," Golda Meir Center for Political Leadership, accessed February 19, 2018, http://msudenver.edu/golda/goldameir /goldaquotes/.

12. Alexander Zvielli and Calev Ben-David, "Abba Eban, Father of Israeli Diplomacy, Dies at 87," *Jerusalem Post*, November 18, 2002, reposted by Facts of Israel, accessed Febraury 19, 2018, http://www.factsofisrael.com/blog/archives /000491.html.

13. Donald Grey Barnhouse, *Genesis: A Devotional Exposition*, vols. 1 and 2 (Grand Rapids: Zondervan, 1973), quoted in David Guzik, "Genesis 12—God's Call of Abram; Abram in Egypt," Enduring Word Bible Commentary, accessed February 12, 2018, https://enduringword.com/commentary/genesis-12/.

Chapter 7: Rapture: The Great Mystery

1. Charles Caldwell Ryrie, *Basic Theology: A Popular Systematic Guide to Understanding Biblical Truth* (Chicago: Moody, 1999), 462.

2. Ryan Jones, "Netanyahu to Hold Official Bible Studies," Israel Today, December 11, 2011, http://www.israeltoday.co.il/NewsItem/tabid/178/nid/23040 /Default.aspx.

3. Robert Andrews, *Famous Lines: A Columbia Dictionary of Familiar Quotations* (New York: Columbia UP, 1997), 256.

Chapter 8: Rapture: The Great Gathering

1. Arnold G. Fruchtenbaum, *The Footsteps of Messiah*, rev. ed. (Tustin, Calif.: Ariel Ministries, 2003), 151, quoted in "14.7. The Church and the Book of Revelation Commentary—A Testimony of Jesus Christ," Bible Study Tools, accessed

February 19, 2018, www.biblestudytools.com/commentaries/revelation/related
-topics/the-church-and-the-book-of-revelation.html.

Chapter 9: The Antichrist: The Man of Lawlessness

1. United Nations Framework Convention on Climate Change, "A Summary of the Kyoto Protocol," United Nations, November 29, 2007, http://unfccc.int/kyoto_protocol /background/items/2879.php. See also "Kyoto Protocol Fast Facts," CNN, March 24, 2017, http://www.cnn.com/2013/07/26/world/kyoto-protocol-fast-facts/index.html.

2. Madison Park, "Obama: No Greater Threat to Future than Climate Change," CNN, January 21, 2015, http://www.cnn.com/2015/01/21/us/climate -change-us-obama/.

3. Pope Francis, "Encyclical Letter Laudato Si' of the Holy Father Francis on Care for Our Common Home," Libreria Editrice Vaticana (Vatican Publishing House), May 24, 2015, http://w2.vatican.va/content/francesco/en/encyclicals/documents /papa-francesco_20150524_enciclica-laudato-si.html.

4. Bradford Richardson, "Pope Francis Calls Climate Change a 'Sin,'" *Washington Times*, September 1, 2016, http://www.washingtontimes.com/news/2016 /sep/1/pope-francis-calls-climate-change-sin/.

Chapter 10: The Antichrist: Rolling Out the Red Carpet

1. "Real Politics, at Last?" *Economist*, October 28, 2004, http://www.economist .com/node/3332056#print?Story_ID=3332056.

2. Bruno Waterfield, "EU Elections 2014: Why Planet EU Is Stranger than Fiction," *Telegraph*, May 13, 2014, http://www.telegraph.co.uk/news/worldnews/eur ope/eu/10823000/EU-elections-2014-Why-Planet-EU-is-stranger-than-fiction.html.

3. Council for Cultural Co-operation, "Europe: Many Tongues, One Voice," Council of Europe, 1992, Pinterest, December 3, 2016, www.pinterest.com/pin /375135843946147782.

4. Becket Adams, "Double-Take: EU 'Tolerance' Poster Includes the Cross, the Star of David, And . . . Wait, What Is That?" TheBlaze, October 19, 2012, http:// www.theblaze.com/news/2012/10/19/double-take-eu-tolerance-poster-includes -the-cross-the-star-of-david-and-wait-what-is-that.

5. Michael Wintle, *Europa and the Bull, Europe, and European Studies: Visual Images as Historical Source Material* (Amsterdam: Vossiuspers UvA, 2004), 22.

6. The Editors of Encyclopædia Britannica, "Europa," Encyclopædia Britannica, February 22, 2016, https://www.britannica.com/topic/Europa-Greek-mythology.

7. Tracy L. Schmidt, ed., *Standard Catalog of World Paper Money, General Issues, 1368–1960*, (Blue Ash, Ohio: F + W Media, Inc., 2016), 562.

8. "Europa Series of Euro Banknotes," European Central Bank, February 19, 2018, http://www.ecb.europa.eu/euro/banknotes/europa/html/index.en.html.

9. John MacArthur, *The MacArthur Bible Commentary* (Nashville: Thomas Nelson Inc., 2005), 1997.

10. New World Encyclopedia contributors, "Albert Speer," New World Encyclopedia, February 24, 2016, http://www.newworldencyclopedia.org/p/index.php ?title=Albert_Speer&oldid=994184.

11. "The Mysterious World and History of the Knights Templar," Beyond Science, July 25, 2017, http://www.beyondsciencetv.com/2017/07/25/the-mysterious -world-and-history-of-the-knights-templar/.

12. Anne Gilmour-Bryson, *The Trial of the Templars in the Papal State and the Abruzzi* (Vatican City, Biblioteca Apostolica Vaticana, 1982), 15.

13. Nash Jenkins, "Hundreds Gather for Unveiling of Satanic Statue in Detroit," *Time*, July 27, 2015, time.com/3972713/detroit-satanic-statue-baphomet/.

14. Isabel Hernández, "Meet the Man Who Started the Illuminati," *National Geographic History*, July/August 2016, https://www.nationalgeographic.com /archaeology-and-history/magazine/2016/07-08/profile-adam-weishaupt-illumi nati-secret-society/.

15. Ibid.

16. The Editors of Encyclopædia Britannica, "Illuminati," Encyclopædia Britannica, September 20, 2017, https://www.britannica.com/topic/illuminati-desig nation#ref1250318.

17. Ibid.

18. Ibid.

19. The Editors of Encyclopædia Britannica, "Freemasonry," Encyclopædia Britannica, June 8, 2017, http://www.britannica.com/topic/order-of-Freemasons.

20. Juan Carlos Ocaña, "The Origins 1919–1939," The History of the European Union: The European Citizenship, February 12, 2018, http://www.historia siglo20.org/europe/anteceden.htm.

21. Juan Carlos Ocaña, "Chronology," The History of the European Union: The European Citizenship, February 12, 2018, http://www.historiasiglo20.org /europe/cronologia.htm.

22. EUR-Lex, "Treaty Establishing the European Coal and Steel Community, ECSC Treaty," EUR-Lex: Access to European Union Law, October 15, 2010, http: //eur-lex.europa.eu/legal-content/EN/TXT/?uri=uriserv%3Axy0022.

23. EUR-Lex, "Treaty of Rome (EEC)," EUR-Lex: Access to European Union Law, March 14, 2017, http://eur-lex.europa.eu/legal-content/EN/TXT/?uri=uriserv %3Axy0023.

24. Juan Carlos Ocaña, "The Single European Act and the Road toward the Treaty of the European Union (1986–1992)," The History of the European Union: The European Citizenship, February 12, 2018, http://www.historiasiglo20.org /europe/acta.htm.

25. Juan Carlos Ocaña, "The Treaty of Maastricht (1992)," The History of the European Union: The European Citizenship, February 12, 2018, http://www .historiasiglo20.org/europe/maastricht.htm.

26. Juan Carlos Ocaña, "The Treaty of Amsterdam (1997)," The History of the European Union: The European Citizenship, February 12, 2018, http://www .historiasiglo20.org/europe/amsterdam.htm.

27. "The Lisbon Treaty: A Brief Guide," European Union External Action, April 22, 2010, https://eeas.europa.eu/sites/eeas/files/eu_lisbon_treaty_guide_22 _04_2010.pdf.

28. Ben Chu, "Brexit to Result in a Sharp Slowdown in UK Economic Growth, OECD Predicts," *Independent*, November 28, 2017, http://www.independent.co

.uk/news/business/news/brexit-oecd-economic-forecast-paris-gdp-eu-european
-union-a8079586.html.

Chapter 11: Days of Ezekiel 36–37: What Was and What Is

1. Peter Spence, "The World Is Defenceless against the Next Financial Crisis, Warns BIS," *Telegraph*, June 28, 2015, http://www.telegraph.co.uk/finance/economics/11704051/The-world-is-defenseless-against-the-next-financial-crisis-warns-BIS.html.

2. Kathryn Schulz, "The Really Big One," *New Yorker*, July 20, 2015, http://www.newyorker.com/magazine/2015/07/20/the-really-big-one.

3. Dario Leone, "Operation Opera: How 8 Israeli F-16s Destroyed an Iraqi Nuclear Plant 33 Years Ago Today," Aviationist, July 7, 2014, https://theaviationist.com/2014/06/07/operation-opera-explained/.

4. Gili Cohen, "For Sale: 40 Israeli F-16 Fighter Jets with History," *Haaretz*, December 27, 2016, http://www.haaretz.com/israel-news/security-aviation/.premium.MAGAZINE-for-sale-40-israeli-f-16-fighter-jets-with-history-1.5478910.

5. UNSCR, "Resolution 487: Iraq-Israel," United Nations Security Council Resolutions, June 19, 1981, http://unscr.com/en/resolutions/487.

6. "Cheney to Israel: Thanks for Destroying Iraqi Reactor; Will U.S. Take 10 Years to Accept Israeli Stance on Peace?" Center for Security Policy, October 30, 1991, http://www.centerforsecuritypolicy.org/1991/10/30/cheney-to-israel-thanks-for-destroying-iraqi-reactor-will-u-s-take-10-years-to-accept-israeli-stance-on-peace-2/.

7. David Makovsky, "The Silent Strike," *New Yorker*, September 17, 2012, http://www.newyorker.com/magazine/2012/09/17/the-silent-strike.

8. "Operation Moses—Aliyah of Ethiopian Jewry (1984)," Ministry of Aliyah and Integration, accessed February 19, 2018, http://www.moia.gov.il/English/FeelingIsrael/AboutIsrael/Pages/mivtzaMoshe.aspx.

9. Joel Brinkley, "Ethiopian Jews and Israelis Exult as Airlift Is Completed," *New York Times*, May 26, 1991, http://www.nytimes.com/1991/05/26/world/ethiopian-jews-and-israelis-exult-as-airlift-is-completed.html.

Chapter 12: Days of Ezekiel 38–39: What Is and What Will Be

1. Adam Lebor, "Exodus: Europe's Jews Are Fleeing Once Again," *Newsweek*, July 29, 2014, http://www.newsweek.com/2014/08/08/exodus-why-europes-jews-are-fleeing-once-again-261854.html.

2. Joseph Benson, "Ezekiel 38," *Commentary of the Old and New Testaments* (New York: T. Carlton & J. Porter, 1857), Bible Hub, accessed February 19, 2018, http://www.biblehub.com/commentaries/benson/ezekiel/38.htm.

3. Robin Wright, "'Death to America!' and the Iran Deal," *New Yorker*, July 30, 2015, http://www.newyorker.com/news/news-desk/death-to-america-and-the-iran-deal.

4. Michael B. Kelley, "The Stuxnet Virus at Iran's Nuclear Facility Was Planted by an Iranian Double Agent," *Business Insider*, April 13, 2012, http://www.businessinsider.com/stuxnet-virus-planted-by-iranian-double-agent-2012-4.

5. Ellen Nakashima, Greg Miller, and Julie Tate, "U.S., Israel Developed Flame Computer Virus to Slow Iranian Nuclear Efforts, Officials Say," *Washington Post*, June 19, 2012, http://www.washingtonpost.com/world/national-security/us-israel-developed-computer-virus-to-slow-iranian-nuclear-efforts-officials-say/2012/06/19/gJQA6xBPoV_story.html?utm_term=.c0a25a55a7ba.

6. Michael Warren, "Kerry Scolds: In One-State Solution, 'Israel Can Either Be Jewish or Democratic. It Cannot Be Both,'" *Weekly Standard*, December 28, 2016, http://www.weeklystandard.com/michael-warren/kerry-scolds-in-one-state-solution-israel-can-either-be-jewish-or-democratic-it-cannot-be-both.

Amir Tsarfati was born in Israel and has lived there most of his life. Since fulfilling his mandatory service in the Israeli Defense Force, he has continued as a major in the IDF Reserve. Amir has been a tour guide in Israel for the last twenty years, serving as chief tour guide of Sar El Tours (2004–2010) and CEO of Sar El Tours and Conferences (2010–2012). In 2001, he became founder and president of Behold Israel—a nonprofit organization that provides worldwide real-time access to reliable sources of news and information about Israel from within the powerful context of Bible history and prophecy.

Amir is married to Miriam, and together they have four children, the oldest of whom has begun his service in the IDF. Amir's home overlooks the valley of Megiddo, Armageddon, which is a constant reminder of the call that the Lord has placed on him to teach from the Bible God's plans for the end times.